THE DOMINICAN REPUBLIC
Beyond The Lighthouse

James Ferguson

THE DOMINICAN REPUBLIC
Beyond The Lighthouse

James Ferguson

For Catriona

LATIN AMERICA|BUREAU

First published in 1992 by the Latin America Bureau (Research and Action) Ltd,
1 Amwell Street, London EC1R 1UL

A CIP catalogue record for this book is available from the British Library

ISBN 0 906156 64 5 PBK
ISBN 0 906156 65 3 HBK

Written by James Ferguson
Edited by Duncan Green

Cover painting by G. Leveque
Cover design by Andy Dark

Typeset, printed and bound by Russell Press, Nottingham NG7 3HN
Trade distribution in UK by Central Books, 99 Wallis Road, London E9 5LN
Distribution in North America by Monthly Review Press, 122 West 27th Street, New York, NY 10001

Contents

Acronyms

ADP	*Asociación Dominicana de Profesores* Dominican Teachers' Association
AFL-CIO	American Federation of Labor-Congress of Industrial Organizations
AMD	*Asociación Médica Dominicana* Dominican Medical Association
BS	*Bloque Socialista* Socialist Bloc
CARICOM	Caribbean Common Market
CDE	*Corporación Dominicana de Electricidad* Dominican Electricity Corporation
CEA	*Consejo Estatal del Azúcar* State Sugar Council
CEDEE	*Centro Dominicano de Estudios de la Educación* Dominican Centre of Education Studies
CGT	*Confederación General del Trabajo* General Confederation of Labour
CLP	*Comité de Lucha Popular* Popular Struggle Committee
CONAMUCA	*Confederación Nacional de Mujeres Campesinas* National Confederation of Peasant Women
COP	*Colectivo de Organizaciones Populares* Collective of Popular Organisations
COPADEBA	*Comités para la Defensa de los Derechos Barriales* Neighbourhood Rights Defence Committees
CORDE	*Corporación Dominicana de Empresas Estatales* Dominican State Corporation
CRESDIP	*Centre de Recherches Sociales et de Diffusion Populaire (Haiti)* Social Research and Popular Distribution Centre
CUT	*Central Unitaria de Trabajadores* United Confederation of Workers
GRIPAC	*Grupo de Investigación para la Acción Comunitaria*

	Research Group for Community Action
IAD	*Instituto Agrario Dominicano*
	Dominican Agrarian Institute
IADB	Inter American Development Bank
IFZ	Industrial Free Zone
IMF	International Monetary Fund
IMOC	*Instituto del Movimiento Obrero,*
	Campesino y Popular
	Labour, Peasant and Popular Movement
	Institute
INESPRE	*Instituto para la Estabilización de los Precios*
	Institute for Price Stabilisation
JCE	*Junta Central Electoral*
	Central Electoral Board
MAAG	Military Aid and Advisory Group
MCI	*Movimiento Campesino Independiente*
	Independent Peasant Movement
MODERNO	*Movimiento de Renovación Nacional*
	National Renovation Movement
NACLA	North American Congress on Latin
	America
OAS	Organization of American States
PCD	*Partido Comunista Dominicano*
	Dominican Communist Party
PLD	*Partido de la Liberación Dominicana*
	Dominican Liberation Party
PQD	*Partido Quisqueyano Demócrata*
	Quisqueyan Democratic Party
PRD	*Partido Revolucionario Dominicano*
	Dominican Revolutionary Party
PR	*Partido Reformista*
	Reformist Party (becomes PRSC in 1984)
PRI	*Partido Revolucionario Independiente*
	Independent Revolutionary Party
PRSC	*Partido Reformista Social Cristiano*
	Social Christian Reformist Party
PTD	*Partido de los Trabajadores Dominicanos*
	Dominican Workers' Party
UCN	*Unión Cívica Nacional*
	National Civic Union
USAID	United States Agency for International
	Development

The Dominican Republic in Brief

Statistics

Area	48,734 sq kms
Population	7 million (mid-1990 estimate)
Growth	3.2% (1982-9)
Capital	Santo Domingo (2.2 million)
Other cities	Santiago de los Caballeros (467,000)
	La Vega (189,000)
	San Francisco de Macorís (162,000)
Urban population	58% (1990)

The People

Origins	Mixed European-African 75%
	Afro-Caribbean 10%
	Others 15%
Language	Spanish
Religion	Roman Catholic 90%

The Economy

Gross Domestic Product	US$6.7 billion (1989)
Per capita GDP	US$957 (1989)
Real GDP growth	0.7% (1988); 4.1% (1989); -5.1% (1990)

GDP by sector (1989)	Manufacturing 15.6%
	Agriculture 14.1%
	Commerce 13.9%
	Construction 10.9%
	Financial services 9.7%
	Government sector 8.3%
	Transport and communications 7.5%
	Mining 3.9%
	Electricity, gas and water 1.6%
	Other 14.5%

Exports (1990)	US$734.7 million
Imports (1990)	US$1,792.9 million
Trade balance (1990)	-US$1,058.2 million
Tourism earnings (1990)	US$900 million
Current account (1990)	-US$58.6 million

Principal exports	Ferronickel; sugar; gold; coffee; cocoa
Principal imports	Intermediate goods; capital goods; consumer goods; oil
Main trading partners:	
exports	US (61%); EC (18.9%)
imports	US (43%); Venezuela (12%); EC (11.8%); Japan(10.6%)
Total external debt	US$4.6 billion (1990)
Per capita debt	US$657 (1990)
Debt service as % of exports of goods and services (1989)	12.9%
Inflation	45% (1989); 100% (1990); 3% (1991 forecast)
Exchange rate *peso*/US dollar	2.9 (1986); 6.10 (1988); 8.3 (1990); 12.67 (December 1991)

The Society

Unemployment (official)	30%
Life expectancy	66 years
Literacy	69%
Infant mortality	70/1,000
% of population with access to electricity	37%
Population per doctor	1,760

Sources: Economist Intelligence Unit; International Monetary Fund; Latin America Monitor; Inter-American Development Bank; World Bank

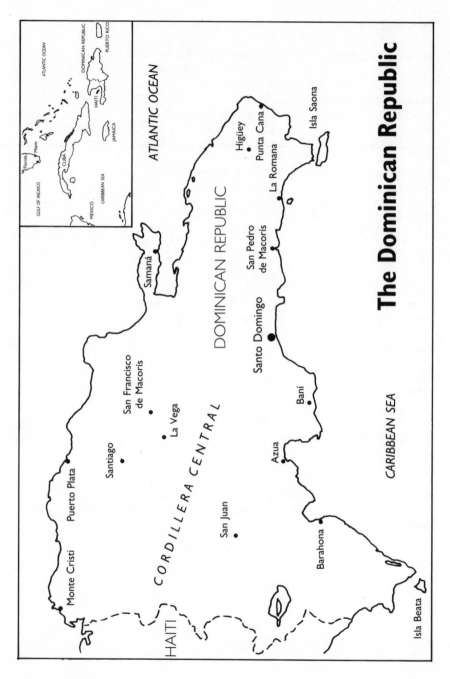

The Dominican Republic

x

Introduction

'The crisis lies precisely in the fact that the old is dying and the new cannot be born; in this period of transition appears a great variety of morbid symptoms.' Antonio Gramsci.

The word crisis has all but lost its meaning in the Dominican Republic. The crisis — political, economic, social — has been so ever-present since the late 1970s that the lexicon of political catastrophe has almost become redundant through overuse. For how long can a country be 'on the brink of collapse', 'in terminal decline' or 'close to bankruptcy'?

The Dominican Republic, described by two US writers as 'both the first and the most typical Latin American state' (Wiarda and Kryzanek 1982:26) has certainly suffered most of the problems which afflicted the region during the 1980s. A mounting debt problem, an IMF-prescribed 'stabilisation' programme and a series of devaluations have combined with falling commodity prices — notably that of sugar — to reduce government spending, push up prices and increase unemployment.

In the 1990s the Dominican Republic faces the threat of further marginalisation as Europe and the US turn their attention increasingly to eastern Europe and its investment potential. In an age of free trade agreements and economic blocs, the country, like other Latin American and Caribbean states, is particularly vulnerable. As the US, Canada and Mexico construct their free trade agreement, the Dominican Republic seems set to lose what comparative advantage it has enjoyed within the US market during the 1980s.

In parallel with the economic malaise is a political crisis which has developed through several stages since the early 1960s. After the assassination of the dictator Trujillo, a long-awaited democratic transition was aborted by a military coup, leading to civil war and a full-scale US invasion in 1965. Political life still bears the scars of these traumatic events. A series of highly dubious elections has further undermined the country's experience of democracy. The post-Trujillo period has been dominated by a politician who was once the dictator's chosen president and who won his sixth term of office at the age of 83. Since that election the Dominican Republic has seen a series of general strikes, demonstrations and violent confrontations between protestors and the military.

In human terms the crisis takes many forms. Every day the Dominican press contains stories of suffering and despair. In June 1991, for instance, it was reported that 16 parents from the mountain town of Jarabacoa had been arrested and charged with selling their children to foreigners. Thousands of Dominicans each year are desperate enough to try the infamous Mona crossing, crowding into precarious wooden fishing boats in order to reach the 'promised land' of Puerto Rico. Most are repatriated; some never arrive and are drowned in the attempt. In Santo Domingo, meanwhile, the poorest of the poor are unceremoniously evicted from their slums as the government seeks to beautify the capital for tourists. Many of these people are simply dumped on the outskirts of the city and left to start again.

For many Dominicans daily life is a struggle against rising prices and deteriorating services. Visitors returning to the country are struck by the dramatic collapse of the country's infrastructure. Power cuts have become a fact of life, and most wealthy individuals and businesses have had to install private generators. Spending on health and education has continued to drop, leading to decaying buildings and a demoralised workforce. In the countryside, lack of land, credit and opportunities is driving growing numbers of people into the shantytowns of Santo Domingo and beyond.

As the Dominican Republic prepares for the 1992 quincentennial celebrations it has received unwelcome attention from the world's media. Not only has the folly of the Columbus lighthouse (estimated by some sources to have cost as much as US$250 million) and other construction been criticised, but the nature of the 'beautification' programme, with its forcible evictions, has caused considerable controversy. Even more serious have been the many allegations from human rights organisations concerning the exploitation of Haitian labour in the Dominican Republic. The issue of Haitians inside the Dominican Republic came to a climax in June 1991 when the Dominican government ordered the deportation of all 'illegal' Haitians. The resulting action by the Dominican security forces, together with further allegations of human rights abuses, did little to improve traditionally strained relations between the two countries.

Between the Old and the New

In the thirty years since the death of Trujillo, the Dominican Republic has undergone profound economic and social change. The once-dominant sugar industry has staggered from one disaster to another, saved only by occasional rises in the world sugar price and dependent upon cheap labour from Haiti. In its place are appearing the new agro-industries, offering pineapples, vegetables and flowers to the US market. As the traditional smallholding peasantry declines, there are growing numbers of new entrepreneurs, supported by foreign investment and modern technology.

The Dominican Republic has also entered into the Caribbean tourist industry with dramatic results. Within ten years the country has become one of the leading regional destinations, receiving almost 1,500,000 visitors in 1989. This growth has been matched by an influx of so-called Industrial Free Zones, complexes of factories which manufacture goods almost exclusively for export to the US and European markets. In both cases, the attraction for foreign investors lies in the low wages paid to Dominicans who work in tourist resorts or assembly plants.

These developments have changed the Dominican Republic's economic profile out of all recognition. Now increasingly an urban society engaged in service industries, the country is less dependent on sugar and other agricultural exports and more involved in supplying cheap labour to offshore export industries. A new generation of business operators and investors has emerged to challenge the traditional land-owning oligarchy. The old icons of status — land, European ancestry, connections with the best families — now have to compete with US-inspired technology and values.

Changes in the Dominican economy have led to changes in the country's social structure. With the decline in traditional agriculture and the growth of urban manufacturing industries, many have deserted dying villages in search of new opportunities in the city. The US, too, offers the prospect of work and self-advancement, and growing numbers of Dominicans try each year — legally or illegally — to join the exile communities of New York or Miami. The monthly remittance cheque sent from relatives in the US is now the main source of income for large numbers of Dominican families.

Not that economic change has led to better conditions for the majority of poor Dominicans. Instead, the move towards service industries and export-led development has been based precisely on the availability of cheap, and for the most part unorganised, labour. Moreover, the chronic economic problems surrounding the country's foreign debt and the adjustment measures taken to counter them have affected the poor directly and disastrously.

Yet, if the Dominican economy has undergone a profound transformation, the same cannot be said of the country's political system. Here, little has changed since the end of the Trujillo dictatorship. The same individuals and the same issues dominate Dominican politics as they did in the 1960s. The cult of *personalismo* continues to reign supreme, and the main political parties remain vehicles for the ambitions of their leaders and their would-be successors.

The traditional political practices of clientilism and corruption survive intact. Political power is still widely seen as a route to financial gain. The large Dominican state sector, the legacy of Trujillo's personal empire, offers ample opportunities for political patronage and favours, while the military and police are reportedly involved in many lucrative sidelines.

The democratic transition which the ephemeral 1963 presidency of Juan Bosch promised has never really materialised. Although periodic elections have occurred, they have been marred by fraud. When the opposition Revolutionary Dominican Party (PRD) was 'allowed' to win the election of 1978, the conditions imposed upon it by the outgoing administration and the military were such as to render it impotent. Nor did the two successive PRD governments significantly reform the political system, while the economy sank deeper into crisis.

Dominican politics appear anachronistic, frozen in time, irrelevant to the real changes happening in the country. The return to power of the 83-year-old President Balaguer in 1990 seemed to symbolise the huge distance between the political establishment and the overwhelmingly young Dominican population. That distance breeds disillusionment and apathy, but also anger as government policies openly prioritise foreign investment over spending on health or education. The growth of the popular movement is a reflection of such anger and also of the failure of the traditional parties to mobilise the poorest sectors of Dominican society.

The contradiction between economic change and political stagnation is one of the factors underlying the Dominican crisis. Most Dominicans have lost faith in the political system and are cynical about what it can deliver. High abstention rates in the 1990 election meant that President Balaguer retained power with the support of only 18 per cent of the electorate. Consequently, many see the government — and the system as a whole — as operating without real legitimacy.

The End of an Era?

The extraordinary longevity of a generation of Dominican politicians has determined the last 30 years of the country's history. Some sort of change, however, is imminent, since both President Balaguer and his long-time rival, Juan Bosch, cannot continue for very much longer as leaders of their parties. It remains to be seen whether their departure will signal a transformation within the political system or whether their successors will merely continue in the same fashion.

Whatever the outcome of the succession process, there is insistent pressure from many quarters for more radical political change. Both the new generation of Dominican entrepreneurs and technocrats and the popular organisations are disaffected with the existing political parties and the system which they perpetuate. The authoritarian political culture which has evolved out of the Trujillo dictatorship appears increasingly discredited, capable only of confrontation with the majority of poor Dominicans.

At the end of 1991 it seemed probable that the next Dominican government would be led by the veteran social democrat, José Francisco Peña Gómez. Elections, constitutionally due by 1994, may take place earlier as President Balaguer's grasp on power weakens. If Peña Gómez does win, it offers the opposition PRD another opportunity to move the country away from the traditional practices of Dominican ruling parties. In its last period in power, it signally failed to achieve any such reforms.

Perhaps more crucial in the long term is the future of the Dominican popular movement. This myriad of local organisations has the vitality and commitment to democratic change so lacking in the established parties. However, it also has a tendency towards institutional instability and fragmentation. Although able to paralyse the country with a series of locally organised strikes, it is incapable of formulating a long-term political programme. Even though the political establishment remains in deep crisis, the popular movement seems unable to grasp the initiative and change the terrain of political debate.

'What is certain is that today all the forces of political reform have failed, democratic institutions have been unable to strengthen themselves, and worse still, society and the political system find themselves on the edge of disintegration' (Catrain 1991:17). Such pessimism is common among political analysts, both in the Dominican Republic and abroad. For as long as the old political order survives it will perhaps be justified. But how long the old order can survive in the face of sweeping changes in the region and the country itself is an open question.

1

Identity Crisis

In the Dominican Republic today the memory of Juan Pablo Duarte is widely venerated. Streets, schools and hospitals bear his name; his face appears on the country's one *peso* bank note. Duarte has become a Dominican icon, symbolising the country's struggle for independence and nationhood. Together with Ramón Mella and Francisco del Rosario Sánchez, Duarte was the leader of a secret nationalist organisation — *la Trinitaria* — which seized power from the occupying Haitian army on 27 February 1844. On that date the Dominican Republic was baptised and first came into being as an independent state.

Duarte's statue now watches over one of the busiest intersections of central Santo Domingo. Around it stand the high-rise offices and shopping malls of the capital city's business quarter. At its centre, surrounded by *barrios* and slums, Santo Domingo flaunts the modern veneer of 'Americanisation' common to most Latin American capitals. But here the cultural presence of the US is particularly strong; alongside the main streets named after Duarte, Mella and Simón Bolívar are the Avenida George Washington, the Avenida Abraham Lincoln, the Avenida John F. Kennedy.

Santo Domingo's architecture reflects its mixed political and cultural influences. The old colonial quarter, with its narrow streets, churches and whitewashed one-storey houses is a relic of Spanish rule. Here tourists can see the first university built in the Americas and an early 16th-century palace constructed by Diego Columbus, 17 years after his father, Christopher, first landed on the island he named Hispaniola. The modern city, mostly built in the 1960s, is comprised of apartment blocks, hotels and offices in a US-style grid system of wide boulevards. The more distant *barrios* resemble those of any other Latin American or large Caribbean city.

The conflict between Spanish, US and Latin American influence is evident at every level of Dominican life. The government has used the 500th anniversary of Columbus's arrival in Hispaniola to promote the idea of the country's *hispanidad* or Spanishness. Travel agents selling holidays in Spain refer to the *madre patria* (motherland), while the Dominican elite prides itself on its aristocratic European ancestry. Yet most Dominicans feel a stronger attraction to the US and the economic opportunities it seems to offer. According to the US embassy in Santo Domingo, over one million Dominicans live in New York, Miami and other cities and many more try, mostly illegally, to join them each year. North American consumer goods and media images abound: US rock competes with the local pop music, *merengue*, on the radio stations; cars, clothes and food are designed for US tastes; the national sport is baseball.

Relations with other Caribbean countries are problematic. The Dominican Republic has long tended to see itself as Latin American rather than Caribbean, and neighbouring states have resented the way in which it tends to side with South and Central American countries in such international forums as the United Nations. But the Dominican government is now eager to join the Caribbean Common Market (CARICOM), dominated by the English-speaking nations of the region, and a new spirit of regional collaboration is in vogue. Meanwhile, the Dominican Republic looks to other Spanish-speaking territories — Venezuela, Costa Rica, Puerto Rico, Cuba — for trade links and cooperation.

The country's closest neighbour, however, is Haiti, which shares the island of Hispaniola with the Dominican Republic. With a radically different history, language and set of cultural traditions, Haiti inspires fear and dislike among many Dominicans. It has also supplied the Dominican Republic with cheap labour and lucrative trading opportunities for as long as the two modern nations have existed. Relations between the two countries are complex and frequently volatile, a situation exacerbated by their geographical proximity.

The Dominican Republic has always struggled to define its own identity. Invaded twice by the US, occupied for 22 years by Haiti and subject to intermittent colonial rule from Spain, the country's independence has been frequently violated and compromised. Nationhood is a relatively recent concept; full and lasting independence was not achieved until 1865 after the country had asked the Spanish colonial authorities to return. Outside interests have had a disproportionate influence on the Dominican Republic's economy as well as its political direction. The first Spanish colonialists were principally interested in gold, which they sent back to Europe. US companies were behind the growth of the sugar industry in the late

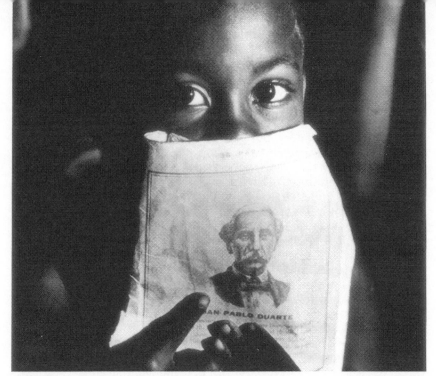

Juan Pablo Duarte... 'A Dominican icon'. (Roger La Brucherie)

19th and early 20th centuries. More recently, Korean, Japanese and Taiwanese companies have joined US multinationals in the new manufacturing and information technology industries based in the Industrial Free Zones. All too often, the Dominican Republic has been literally a state for sale.

Gulf & Western

One of the more bizarre features of the booming Dominican tourist industry is a mock medieval Italian village, perched in the hills behind the eastern sugar town of La Romana. Altos de Chavón, described in the publicity brochures as an 'international artists' village', is an elaborate parody of an idealised European setting, where an apartment can cost US$275 per day. Altos de Chavón was reputedly the brainchild of Charles Bluhdorn, the President of the US multinational, Gulf & Western, who intended it as 'the living expression of the cultural and historical values of the Dominican people'. The village's history is in reality less exalted.

In July 1967 Gulf & Western, a fast-growing conglomerate with interests in cinema, transport and agro-industries, took over the

US-owned South Puerto Rico Sugar Company and with it 276,218 acres of land around La Romana. This made the company the largest private landowner in the Dominican Republic, controlling eight per cent of the country's arable land. Gulf & Western continued sugar production at the La Romana refinery but also diversified rapidly into banking, finance, transport, agro-chemicals and tourism within the Dominican Republic. In 1969 the company signed a 30-year agreement with the Dominican government, allowing it to open and manage an industrial park next to its golf course outside La Romana. Enjoying generous tax concessions, Gulf & Western built the installation with its own subsidiary companies and attracted 24 further businesses, a third of them also Gulf & Western subsidiaries, to La Romana. The industrial park, like the hotel complexes, was — and remains — surrounded by barbed wire fences and patrolled by armed guards. La Romana had become a state within a state.

In the 1980s Gulf & Western's annual turnover was larger that the Dominican Republic's Gross Domestic Product. Whereas the sugar industry and particularly the state-owned sections of it were in crisis, Gulf & Western had made large profits from sugar. An especially lucrative sideline was dealing in the sugar futures market. After a verbal agreement between Bluhdorn and the Dominican government, Gulf & Western speculated with Dominican state-sector sugar on the futures market, with the government promised a 60 per cent share of profits. According to Roger Plant (1987:39):

> Selling dear when the price was at its peak, and purchasing cheap when it had begun to fall, Bluhdorn realised an immense profit of US$64,534,126. In accordance with the verbal agreement, $38,721,000 of this amount should have gone to the Dominican government. Only half of it was apparently mentioned to the Dominicans, but even this reduced amount was not at first paid over to them.

It was only after the Dominican government threatened to sue Gulf & Western and a highly incriminating report had been published by the US Securities and Exchanges Commission that the company agreed to an out-of-court settlement. Even then, Gulf & Western did not pay the money, but promised to fund an equivalent amount in projects 'of social value to the country'. One such project was the Altos de Chavón complex, while another was a Miss Universe contest in the Dominican Republic. Thus money owed to the Dominican government went towards paying for a luxury tourist enclave, operated by Gulf & Western.

In January 1985 Gulf & Western sold its Dominican holdings, together with 90,000 acres of sugar-cane in Florida, to a Palm

Beach-based consortium headed by the Fanjul family, for US$240 million. The Fanjuls, emigre Cubans of Arab origin based in Florida, are prominent anti-Castro activists and, according to *Forbes* magazine, 'demibillionaires'. Since their takeover in the Dominican Republic, they have emphasised tourism, gradually abandoning the ailing sugar industry.

Backyard Republic

Gulf & Western is not the only foreign multinational to have made money out of the Dominican Republic. A multitude of North American companies and their subsidiaries operate in the country: Abbott Laboratories, American Airlines, Chase Manhatten, Citibank, Colegate Palmolive, Esso, Falconbridge, Ford, IBM, Texaco, and Xerox. In all, more than 125 US and other foreign firms were estimated to be present by the mid-1980s; others held interests, but were not necessarily officially registered with the Central Bank. Some, such as the oil companies, Alcoa (the aluminium multinational) and the two main Canadian banks have been active in the Dominican Republic since the 1940s and 1950s. More came to the country during the 1960s after the end of Rafael Leonidas Trujillo's 30-year dictatorship, when the Dominican government opened the economy further to foreign investment. During the 1980s,a new rush of US investment took place, when companies flocked to the expanding Industrial Free Zones.

Registered US private investment in the Dominican Republic stood at approximately US$660 million in 1990. Two main factors attract foreign investors: cheap labour and access to otherwise protected markets. According to the Economist Intelligence Unit, hourly wage levels in the Industrial Free Zones were on average US$0.60 in 1988; by 1990, claims Luis Vargas of the Asociación Pro-Fundación Estudios Dominicanos, they had gone down to US$0.35. Furthermore, under the terms of the 1983 Caribbean Basin Initiative, certain goods originating from the Caribbean are entitled to enter the US market duty-free. These two incentives have made the Dominican Republic particularly attractive to US manufacturers and exporters.

The Dominican economy is extraordinarily dependent upon the US market. In 1990 the US accounted for almost 61 per cent of Dominican exports; that same year the Dominican Republic bought 43 per cent of its imported goods from the US. According to Tom Barry *et al* (1984:300), in the mid-1980s US corporations counted on the Dominican market for US$800 million in annual sales. 'A US-sponsored survey found that 1,598 US companies export from the United States more than 10,000 products that are sold in the Dominican

Falcondo

'Capital from the United States, rather than Canada, is behind Falconbridge and Falcondo: Superior Oil of Texas owns controlling interest in Falconbridge, and US-owned Armco is the second largest share-holder of Falcondo after Falconbridge. Although Falcondo has cultivated close relations with the national government, there have been a number of confrontations resulting from the company's failure to pay taxes. In 1975, the government claimed the company was not declaring its profits in order to avoid taxes. Falcondo took three years to answer the government's charges, and the government took three more years to ratify the validity of the tax claim. Responding to the government's repeated complaints that it was not paying enough taxes, Falconbridge insinuated that it might leave the country. But after a couple of very bad years, Falcondo operations picked up in 1983 when oil costs, which account for about 60 per cent of its expenses, started dropping, and Falconbridge has toned down its threats to leave.'

(Barry *et al* 1984:296-7)

Republic'. Even attempts to establish domestic industries to reduce dependency on foreign products have paradoxically led to increased imports. In 1986, Dominican manufacturers imported 60 per cent of their raw materials; this figure did not include imported machinery, oil and containers (Merino 1986:103).

The power and influence exerted by foreign companies and governments in the Dominican Republic have taken many forms. The fate of the country's economy has often been determined not by the Dominican government, but by the boards of multinationals. In 1959, Alcoa opened a bauxite-mining operation in Barahona province and output reached 1,196,000 tons in 1974. In 1982, however, the company unilaterally closed its plant because of low world prices for bauxite, giving the government no say in the decision. Similarly, the Canada-based Falconbridge mining company (known in the Dominican Republic as Falcondo) has often threatened to close its ferronickel mine at Bonao because the government has questioned the levy it pays on exports out of the Dominican Republic. The unexpected Gulf & Western sellout in 1985 also threatened the Dominican economy and the livelihoods of thousands of workers.

The Dominican Republic therefore depends overwhelmingly on the US for its exports and, to a lesser extent, its imports. It depends on foreign investment in agriculture, manufacturing and tourism and looks to North America for the bulk of its tourists. Its main source of bilateral economic aid — US$63 million in 1989, with US$35.2 requested for 1992 — is the US government, and the US military trains and equips its armed forces. The US can use its power to influence every aspect of political and economic life. In early 1991 Washington reacted to a controversy concerning the mistreatment of Haitian workers in the Dominican sugar industry by threatening to impose trade sanctions; the Dominican government stood to lose US$550 million annually in preferential access to the US market. By early 1992 a new threat to the Dominican economy had materialised in the form of the proposed North American Free Trade Agreement between the US, Canada and Mexico. With duties on goods manufactured in Mexico abolished, why, asked the business community, should US investors choose the Dominican Republic?

Fragile Sovereignty

The Dominican Republic's fragile sovereignty is in part a result of its unusual transition to political independence. Unlike other Latin American countries, the Dominican Republic was not born primarily out of a struggle against a colonial European power. Instead, the founders of the modern nation fought firstly against occupation by neighbouring Haiti, which was itself the second country in the Americas (after the US) to win independence. An anti-colonial guerrilla struggle against Spain only followed 20 years later, after the independent Dominicans had asked the Spanish to reestablish colonial rule.

The Dominican independence struggle was therefore less an anti-colonial conflict than an attempt to define a state separate from Haiti, which itself epitomised the region's anti-colonial militancy. As a result, the Dominican Republic has always sought to define itself in terms of its difference from Haiti and this, in turn, has complicated its relationship with other countries.

The island of Hispaniola (its eastern part was known by the indigenous Arawaks as Quisqueya) was first colonised during Columbus' four expeditions to the region (1492-1504). According to today's tourist slogan, it was the 'land that Columbus loved best'. In reality, it was the scene of murderous squabbles between the European settlers, repeated disappointments for Columbus himself and the genocide of the Taino Arawak population. Estimated at half a million in 1492, this population had all but disappeared fifty years later, destroyed by violence and disease.

The 'golden age' of colonial Hispaniola was short-lived. By 1550, the gold which had attracted European settlers was seemingly exhausted and continental South America was a more tempting proposition for colonists. The city of Santo Domingo lost much of its prestige and the island became a neglected colonial outpost, insignificant in comparison to Mexico or Peru. As Spanish interest waned, pirates and buccaneers — principally from France — began to settle permanently in the west of the island. The Spanish tried to evict them and to defend themselves from attack by British pirates (Sir Francis Drake besieged and burned Santo Domingo in 1586), but gradually the first colonial power lost ground to the French. Spanish decline was officially recognised in 1697, when the Treaty of Ryswick ceded the western third of Hispaniola to France after a 12-year war.

France's colony, named Saint Domingue, was for almost a century the most spectacularly successful enterprise in the Americas. Its exports, chiefly sugar, were worth more than those of the entire English Caribbean. Slaves, brought over from Africa, powered Saint Domingue's economy and created its extraordinary wealth. In contrast, the remaining Spanish territory (now known as Santo Domingo) languished, economically and demographically. Only in 1700, after the colonial authorities boosted the population by shipping in settlers from the Canary Islands, did the population reach 100,000 (Bell 1981:20). In French Saint Domingue, on the other hand, more than 500,000 people lived in a smaller area. The economic role of the Spanish east was to provide beef and other products to the French west. While Saint Domingue was a sugar-exporting slave economy, highly valued by the French metropole, Santo Domingo was a sparsely populated ranching economy, largely neglected by colonial Spain and dependent on the market in the neighbouring French colony.

The slave revolt of 1791 in Saint Domingue led to a rapid and confusing series of events in the whole of the island. Initially, the slaves' leader, Toussaint Louverture, formed an alliance with the Spanish colony against the French authorities. When the government in Paris abolished slavery in 1794, however, he turned on his erstwhile allies, and joined the French forces in invading Santo Domingo. In 1795 Spain ceded its colony to the French and Toussaint Louverture became governor of a unified island under French control. With his removal by Napoleon's forces in 1802, the French retained control of Santo Domingo. Meanwhile the slave revolt in Saint Domingue had become a fully fledged war of independence which led to the founding of the state of Haiti in 1804. The French, defeated in their former colony by the army of ex-slaves led by Jean-Jacques Dessalines, therefore kept a foothold in the east part of the island until 1809, when the Spanish, in league with the British, drove them out and reclaimed Santo Domingo.

Spain had shown scant interest in its colony since the 16th century, but from 1809 to 1821 its record of incompetence and indifference earned the colonial administration the title of *la España Boba* (Foolish Spain). Slavery, which the Haitian revolutionaries had abolished in Santo Domingo, was reintroduced and some economic progress initiated by the French was reversed. After 12 years of widespread hunger and maladministration, the population rebelled and deported the Spanish governor. The anti-Spanish leadership had envisaged incorporation into Simón Bolívar's projected *Gran Colombia* federation, but Bolívar never replied to Santo Domingo's proposal. Instead, the following year, President Jean-Pierre Boyer of Haiti led an army, unopposed, into Santo Domingo and declared the island a single republic.

In modern Dominican mythology the ensuing 22-year Haitian occupation was a period of repression and savagery. The alleged mistreatment of the former Spanish colony by the Haitians is still considered a justifiable reason for anti-Haitian feeling and national security concerns in today's Dominican Republic. According to Juan Bosch (1990:83), traditional Dominican historians have falsified the historical truth:

> The works of these historians leave the reader with the impression that the 22 years of Haitian rule in our country were years of savage tyranny, of unbearable crimes and outrages, of great suffering, poverty and ignorance. But when one looks at what first-hand witnesses said of the period, it emerges that nothing happened in the way that these historians would like one to believe.

The majority of the population, claims Bosch, welcomed the Haitian occupation. For the slaves it meant emancipation; for other blacks and *mulattos* it promised a break from the racist hierarchy of Spanish colonialism. Haiti had also at this point a much more developed economy than its neighbour, and incorporation into a single republic offered improved economic conditions for the poor. The poorest sectors of the population did indeed benefit from Haitian rule. Radical land reform broke up many of the largest estates and church-owned land and distributed it to smallholders. Yet, Boyer's authoritarian and militarised regime gradually provoked resentment and opposition. In particular, the populace of the city of Santo Domingo itself disliked the monopoly of political and administrative power held by Haitians and objected to compulsory military service. It was among the urban elite that *la Trinitaria* was formed and grew. When, in 1843, Boyer's unpopularity reached its peak, the nationalist group allied itself with Charles Hérard's anti-Boyer Haitian faction and ended the 22-year occupation. Previously, the nationalist movement had thought of naming the country Spanish Haiti; now, it settled on the Dominican Republic.

State for Sale

The first priority for the independent country was to defend itself against Haiti, which made unsuccessful bids to reoccupy the territory in 1844, 1849 and 1855. After the liberal independence leadership split amidst plotting and factionalism (Duarte was exiled in 1844), a series of *caudillos* or strongmen fought for control of the republic. To several of them it seemed that the easiest — and most lucrative — way of fending off Haitian attack was to offer the newly independent state as a protectorate or colony to a larger power. General Pedro Santana, who ousted Duarte, offered the Samaná peninsula as a military base to both France and Spain. In 1861, after much pleading from Santana, Spain formally reannexed the Dominican Republic. This was an unprecedented event in the history of the Americas. It also proved to be a disaster, as neither the annexationists such as Santana nor Spain seemed to have learnt anything from the previous period of *la España Boba*. Again, Spain governed badly and repressively, showing contempt for its Dominican subjects. Within two years the nationalist movement had taken up arms again, supported by large numbers of peasants who feared that Spain would reintroduce slavery. A three-year guerrilla War of Restoration forced the Spanish authorities to abandon the country to a renewed independence in July 1865.

Even this experience did not deter the rival *caudillos* from attempting to sell or lease the republic to foreign powers. In 1868, President José María Cabral offered the Samaná peninsula to the US for a one million dollar advance and a yearly rent of US$300,000. The veteran strongman, Buenaventura Báez, made a similar proposal the following year, asking Washington to annex the whole country. US President Ulysses S. Grant approved the scheme, and only the US Senate's failure to give it the necessary two-thirds support prevented the Dominican Republic from becoming part of the US.

However, the wishes of the annexationists were eventually to be granted. The 17-year dictatorship of General Ulises Heureaux had bolstered itself with large loans from European and US bankers. When Heureaux was assassinated in 1899 a succession of short-lived governments (22 in 17 years) were unable to control the country politically or economically. Corrupt leaders and governments borrowed freely from European sources, and in 1905 a US consultant estimated the Dominican external debt at US$40 million, most of it owed to European banks and companies. Fearful of European intervention, the US government took over the collection of Dominican customs duties that year, creating a formal receivership in 1907. It paid off the European creditors, reimbursed US banks and handed over the remaining 45 per cent of the total collected to the Dominican government.

Overt US interference merely exacerbated the Dominican crisis. Political pressures from Washington fuelled a further round of coups, revolts and assassinations. In 1915, the US proposed taking over all Dominican finances and replacing the army with a US-trained constabulary. Dominican indignation at the suggestion forced the resignation of the president. On 15 May 1916 the first detachment of US Marines landed at Santo Domingo, beginning an eight-year occupation.

Occupation

Sugar dominates much of the southern Dominican landscape. Around Barahona, La Romana, San Pedro Macorís and Santo Domingo itself the monotonous acres of cane stretch to the horizon, broken only by the occasional sugar-mill or squalid settlement of cane-cutters. Sugar's grip on the country stems from the latter half of the 19th century and the arrival of refugees from the Cuban civil war in the 1870s and the first North American investors; yet it was really the US invasion of 1916 and the subsequent occupation that transformed the Dominican Republic from a subsistence and ranching economy into a vast sugar plantation.

The invasion took place in the name of regional security and according to the Monroe Doctrine of countering European 'interference' in the Americas. The pretext of stopping German expansion in the region, however, was related to a much more tangible benefit for US investors: World War I had all but destroyed the European sugar-beet industry, doubling the world sugar price. As a result, between 1914 and 1920 Dominican sugar production increased by 79 per cent and land was increasingly concentrated in the hands of the large producers. According to Roger Plant, in 1893 a total of 218,000 *tareas* (1 hectare = 15.9 *tareas*) belonged to the sugar mills and sugar-producing farmers; by 1925, the year after the US withdrew, this figure had risen to 2,826,980 *tareas* (Plant 1987:14). That year, 11 of the 21 mills operating belonged to US corporations, and 98 per cent of sugar exports went to the US.

The sugar boom brought parts of the Dominican Republic abruptly into the 20th century. According to Frank Moya Pons (1980:480), the so-called 'Dance of the Millions' paid for the beginnings of a modern urban society:

> During this short period, some towns like Santiago, La Vega, San Pedro de Macorís and Puerto Plata became urban in a true sense. Sugar made of Macorís a city with large houses of reinforced concrete and streetcars in the street to transport passengers. Puerto Plata and Santiago with tobacco and La Vega and Sánchez with cocoa, favoured by the railroads, were also converted into noisy commercial centres where day after day new buildings and stores were erected and the families who had commercial interests became rich overnight.

The US military authorities enacted legislation to help sugar growers take over Dominican land. The 1920 Land Registration Act, reinforcing previous but ineffectual land ownership laws, was designed to break up the communally owned lands (*terrenos comuneros*) and bring them into private ownership. The legislation, by destroying long-standing patterns of land tenure, drove many squatters and communal farmers off the land, adding thousands of hectares to the sugar plantations. This process made fortunes for those Dominican businessmen who simply incorporated these holdings into their properties by obtaining legally recognised land titles. The modern-day dynasties of Santiago, San Pedro de Macorís and Santo Domingo — names such as Bermúdez, Barceló and Espaillat — owe their current prosperity to the US occupation.

At the same time, the 1920 Tariff Act removed protectionist barriers against US food imports, allowing a flood of US foodstuffs and other goods into the country and crippling the nascent Dominican manufacturing sector. Domestic food production declined, a landless rural workforce was created and sugar's short-lived 'Dance of the Millions' tied the Dominican Republic even more firmly to the economic power of the US.

The US occupation resulted in some infrastructural improvements, although these were mostly funded by the Dominican taxpayer (the US authorities had taken control of the 45 per cent of revenues previously granted to the Dominican state) and related to streamlining sugar production and exporting. Initiatives concerning health and education also brought some modest results. But the most enduring legacy of the 1916 invasion was the creation of the Guardia Nacional Dominicana in 1917. Formed to replace the defunct Dominican army, the Guardia Nacional was trained, armed and led by the US army as a counter-insurgency force. Since 1916 the most militant sectors of the

The 'Haitian threat': a cartoon from *Hoy* newspaper, 1991.

Dominican peasantry, particularly those dispossessed by the land legislation, had fought the US occupying forces. In the east especially, the *gavilleros* resisted until 1922 and encountered full-scale military repression, including some of the first-ever bombing raids carried out by the US Air Force (Mariñez 1984:61). The Guardia Nacional was intended to support and eventually replace the US military in the counter-insurgency conflict. This it did, eventually acting as the springboard for the political career of the longest-lasting Dominican dictator, Trujillo.

Alien Nation

'Everything points to the decline of the nation that we once knew... Culture, language, values — all the things that yesterday made up the spiritual frontier — have been submerged by changes in our national identity, transforming our rural culture and the spiritual face of the towns. We are moving further and further away from what we once were, while on top of the ruin of our old selves a new nation is born. With the Haitianisation of the countryside and the Americanisation of the towns acting as alien influences on it, the new nation will create new ways of life, new forms of culture and a new history.' (Núñez 1990:55)

A recent academic analysis of Dominican cultural identity proved to be an unexpected best-seller in Santo Domingo's bookshops. Lamenting the loss of authentic Dominican values and warning of the 'Haitianisation' of the country, the book played on long-standing anxieties about the Dominican Republic's self-image. 'We are', wrote Manuel Núñez, 'a deeply imitative and insecure culture.' Soon after the book was published, yet another crisis in relations between the

Dominican Republic and Haiti erupted. Dominican newspapers were filled with articles and editorials questioning the concept of an authentic national identity and championing the patriotic values of 'Dominicanness'.

'Dominicanness', however, is an elusive and questionable concept, since the inhabitants of today's Dominican Republic reflect the different phases of the country's history and different generations of immigrants. Of the original Quisqueyans, of course, there remains no trace. Instead, there are the descendants of the original Spanish settlers, and of subsequent immigrants from the Canary Islands, Cubans and Puerto Ricans, Italians, Chinese, black North Americans, Jews, Syrian-Lebanese and blacks from the English-speaking Caribbean. To this ethnically diverse population must be added the influence of Haiti, not merely from the 19th-century occupation, but from day-to-day contact ever since.

But for Núñez, as for the editorialists of the Dominican press and many political leaders, Haiti, with its negative image of backwardness, stands in opposition to that which is authentically Dominican. A myth of racial superiority has grown up which paints the Dominican Republic as European, modern and democratic and Haiti as African, archaic and dictatorial. Some Dominicans reject such stereotypes and stress their common cultural roots. Despite their work in trade unions, education and popular organisations, they are a minority.

Such attitudes reflect the long history of foreign interference and dependency experienced by the Dominican Republic. Constantly fearful of its Haitian neighbour and in thrall to the US economy, the country has often found its sense of identity dominated by external forces. While the relics of a fanciful colonial 'golden age' are officially celebrated alongside the feats of the *la Trinitaria*, an alternative view of Dominican history — marked by invasions, occupations and exploitation — exists. The Dominican Republic, wrote Juan Bosch after the second US invasion in 1965, has always been an 'imperial frontier'.

Today, that frontier still exists and shapes much of the political and social life of the country. Now, the borders of Dominican sovereignty are unlikely to be infringed by a gunboat, yet the presence and influence of foreign powers remain no less pervasive. Haiti is seen by many Dominicans as an overpopulated and territorially ambitious neighbour, ready at any moment to reinvade the eastern part of the island. At the same time, the allure of the US, with its promise of economic opportunities, is paralleled by a sense of resentment over the role played by US governments and businesses in the exploitation of the Dominican Republic. As a love-hate relationship, the Dominican view of the US resembles its deeply ambiguous view of itself.

2

Staying Power

On 13 July 1990 Dr Joaquín Balaguer, leader of the Social Christian
Reformist Party (PRSC), was officially declared President of the
Dominican Republic. It was the sixth time that Balaguer had taken up
office, having already served 20 out of the previous 33 years as
President. At 83 years of age, blind from glaucoma and unable to walk
unassisted, the former lawyer and much-published poet had a long
and chequered political career. His sixth term of office, however, was
to start on a farcical note. When opposition members of the chamber
of deputies boycotted the National Assembly's official announcement
of his recent electoral victory, the Assembly failed to reach its required
quorum. For seven hours deputies, senators and the President-elect
fretted impatiently while helicopters were dispatched to ferry loyalist
deputies from outlying districts.

The announcement of Balaguer's victory — by a single percentage
point — came as no surprise to most Dominicans, even though it had
taken two months for the Central Electoral Board (JCE) to confirm the
result. There had been vehement accusations of cheating and
ballot-rigging, most notably from Juan Bosch, the leader of the
opposition Dominican Liberation Party (PLD), but each of Balaguer's
previous electoral victories had been surrounded by similar allegations
and controversy. As the JCE rejected each of the PLD's detailed
allegations it became obvious that Balaguer was going to be
proclaimed victor. The turning-point came when Jimmy Carter, an
observer at the elections, had declared the polling to be fair. With
Carter's influential support, the JCE was able to conclude the electoral
process.

The allegations of electoral fraud — multiple voting, the sale of
cédulas (voter identity cards), voting by theoretically disenfranchised
military personnel, ballot stuffing — were nothing new. Nor were the
leading personalities in the elections themselves. Balaguer's main

opponent, Juan Bosch, himself 80 years old, had been a dominant figure in Dominican politics for almost 50 years and had fought four presidential elections. The third main contender, José Francisco Peña Gómez, candidate of the Dominican Revolutionary Party (PRD), while only 53 years old, was also a veteran of 30 years of political activity. To Dominicans the personalities, policies and controversies seemed all too familiar; voter abstention stood at 45 per cent.

The apathy and cynicism which characterised the 1990 elections turned to anger later. Shortly after the results were announced, the PLD organised a two-day *duelo cívico* (civic mourning) which paralysed much of the country. Subsequently, two general strikes took place, and security forces killed several protestors, while hundreds were arrested. Speaking before the November general strike, President Balaguer threatened to take 'measures that could be called despotic'. In October, ethe Dominican armed forces had pledged their loyalty to the Balaguer government after two weeks of rumours that a coup was imminent. For the next twelve months the country was to be shaken by a series of strikes and protests, aimed at forcing Balaguer's resignation.

A Beacon of Democracy?

In theory, the Dominican Republic is a democratic success story. Between 1962 and 1990 there were seven elections, each contested by several candidates and parties. In a brochure aimed at US investors, the Dominican Republic Investment Council speaks of a 'stable, multiparty, progressive democracy'. Already in 1985 a North American contributor to the influential *Caribbean Review* observed that the Dominican Republic 'appeared to have completed its journey into the ranks of solid democracies', while in 1984 President Ronald Reagan praised the country as a 'beacon for freedom-loving people everywhere'.

The conduct and aftermath of the 1990 elections cast doubt on such a rosy view of Dominican democracy. Instead, Balaguer's sixth term of office began with a series of events which merely confirmed the fragility of the Dominican Republic's democratic credentials. Many of the country's recurring political problems — electoral malpractice, threatened military intervention, repression and violence — were again in evidence. Furthermore, the unchanging *dramatis personae* of the Dominican electoral arena, with Balaguer and Bosch still dominating the contest, raised questions about the internal democracy of the main parties. Equally doubtful was the relevance of two octogenarian presidential candidates to an increasingly youthful electorate.

Observers have often commented on the survival of the *caudillo* tradition in the Dominican political system. The longevity of politicians such as Balaguer and Bosch has reinforced the role of personality at the expense of policy debate. It has also excluded a generation of Dominicans from political power and led to extensive disillusionment with electoralism. The result is an anachronistic political structure which has hardly changed in 30 years. To some extent, this structure is the legacy of historical tradition, culminating with the Trujillo period and its emphasis on the individual power of *el jefe* or boss. It is also rooted in the unsuccessful attempt to build a liberal democracy in the Dominican Republic after the death of Trujillo and the resulting return to authoritarianism and 'strongman' government. The consequences of that failure have bedevilled the country since 1961, creating a sense of permanent crisis.

The Trujillo Dictatorship

When the Marines left in 1924, the US military left behind the Guardia Nacional, a professionalised counter-insurgency force. Within six years the Guardia Nacional's head, one time plantation foreman and petty thief, Rafael Trujillo, had taken power. Like Somoza in Nicaragua, Trujillo used the US-designed security forces to construct a dictatorship, removing opposition and consolidating his personal power.

The Trujillo regime, conclude two US academics, 'was the first in this hemisphere to really merit the label "totalitarian"' (Wiarda and Kryzanek 1982:12). In effect, Trujillo, with his relations and closest supporters, became synonymous with the state, running the country's economic affairs as a family business. Gradually taking over interests in sugar, construction, manufacturing and ranching, the dictator literally made most of the Dominican Republic his own.

At the time of his death, Trujillo was among the ten richest men in the world. His biographer estimates that he owned 1,500,000 acres of productive land and had personal wealth of US$500 million (Crassweller 1966:279).

The Trujillo empire was held in place by a ruthless use of violence and intimidation. Political murders, torture, deportations and blackmail were commonplace. Only one party — the Partido Dominicano — was allowed to operate, funded by a ten per cent levy on state-sector wages. Periodic elections and plebiscites took place and invariably returned Trujillo or his chosen puppet president with overwhelming majorities. The cult of the leader was taken to absurd lengths; statues, portraits and images of Generalissimo Trujillo were everywhere. In 1936 the regime renamed Santo Domingo Ciudad Trujillo.

The US treated the dictatorship with a mixture of friendship and distrust. Trujillo proclaimed himself the most active anti-communist

'It's the Chief's'

'Primarily, Trujillo was no thieving politician, but big business incarnate. Unlike Carías in Honduras, he was not reduced to picking the treasury clean so that nothing remained for roads and schools. His commercial enterprises were of such inordinate magnitude that the government dwindled in importance to a sideline. He had as little temptation to steal directly from the treasury as the president of a steel trust would have to rifle the firm's petty cash box. One diplomat in Ciudad Trujillo summed up to me his observations over several years: "If you try interpreting the setup here in terms of politics, you will get nowhere. It is not a country but a feudal domain. Trujillo is lord of everybody's life and chattels. He is a progressive overlord, concerned about drainage and plumbing. But he is annoyed at having to waste energy putting on an act to convince the imbeciles of the outside world that his feud is a democracy, or for that matter a country at all..."

Like so many Latin American dictators, Trujillo had a weakness for cattle. He had the state bring in blooded bulls to service the peasants' cows at remount stations throughout the country. Like so much in the Dominican Republic, it was not clear just to whom the bulls belonged, the state or Trujillo. You asked the attendants at the remount station and they replied: "Es del Jefe" ("It's the Chief's"). Such a distinction appeared irrelevant to most Dominicans.'
(Krehm 1984:182-3)

in the hemisphere and dutifully declared war against Germany and Japan in December 1941. But his economic megalomania stood in the way of US investments (although he respected the largest US-owned sugar mills), and Trujillo even nationalised some North American interests. A combination of high world sugar prices and domestic austerity policies (wage freezes, heavy taxation, budget cuts), enabled Trujillo to pursue a nationalist economic policy. He paid off the Dominican foreign debt in full, having earlier ended the US customs receivership of 1907, and created the first independent Dominican currency — the *peso* — to replace the US dollar.

In this sense, Trujillo did much to create the idea of Dominican identity, ending the direct administrative role of the US in national affairs. But under Trujillo's control, nationhood became all but inseparable from the cult of the omniscient leader. Trujillo's version of Dominicanness was also largely based on overtly anti-Haitian sentiment and a vision of the country's 'civilising mission'.

Inevitably, Trujillo alienated the traditional Dominican oligarchy and those who resented his monopolisation of wealth. He also lost

Generalissimo Trujillo (second left) confers with Joaquín Balaguer at a military parade, 1958. (Organization of American States)

US support through the excesses of his regime. When, in 1960, he sponsored an assassination attempt on President Rómulo Betancourt of Venezuela, he incurred sanctions from the Organisation of American States and a US ban on Dominican sugar. In the aftermath of the 1959 Cuban revolution, the US also judged Trujillo's old-style dictatorship to be more vulnerable to socialist revolution than a liberal democracy. In the 1930s, according to one apocryphal tale, President Roosevelt, upon being told by the anti-Trujillo US Senator Sumner Welles that the Dominican dictator was a 'son of a bitch' had replied 'I know he's a son of a bitch, but he's *our* son of a bitch'. In the context of the Kennedy administration's struggle against the perceived Cuban threat, such attitudes were no longer fashionable. On 30 May 1961, a group of disgruntled middle-class Dominicans, supported by the CIA, shot Trujillo dead.

Return of the Gunboats

The president at the time of Trujillo's death was Joaquín Balaguer. He had been hand-picked by the Generalissimo, but quickly showed his capacity for political survival by distancing himself from the fallen regime and the rest of the Trujillo family who were trying to hold onto power. With US pressure, a wave of strikes and popular protests, a powerful military and a dearth of established political leadership, the Dominican Republic faced an explosive situation. Seeking to broaden the appeal of his interim government, Balaguer included members of the National Civic Union (UCN), a conservative anti-*trujillista* organisation. An attempted military coup by officers disgruntled at being left out of the interim regime sent Balaguer into exile, while a reformed Council of State pledged to organise elections for 20 December 1962.

The only real political party was the Dominican Revolutionary Party (PRD). Formed by exiled social democrats in 1939, its head was Juan Bosch, better known as a writer than a politician, who had opposed the Trujillo regime while in Cuba, Venezuela and Europe. When Bosch and the PRD leadership returned to the Dominican Republic they found a receptive audience for their message of nationalism and reform. For the first time in Dominican history, the vast majority of people had a taste of democratic freedom and a sense of political power. Campaigning on issues of land reform, job creation and social justice, Bosch easily defeated the UCN's candidate, Viriato Fiallo, winning 64 per cent of the vote. Voter participation stood at more than 90 per cent (Black 1986:31).

'The coup was organised before I took over as President of the Republic' (Bosch 1966:84). So wrote Bosch in the post-mortem of his brief presidency. In the course of the campaign he had made obvious enemies: the church hierarchy which accused him of atheism, the military which was still heavily influenced by the Trujillo regime, and the tiny upper class for which Bosch resurrected the mocking and untranslatable slang term, *tutumpotes*. Nor did the PRD enjoy the uncritical support of the US government, although President Kennedy himself reportedly approved of the PRD's liberal programme of reform. Once in power, moreover, Bosch rapidly lost the popularity which had swept him into office. Despite a liberal constitution, some distribution of land to poor peasants and expanded political freedoms, little was achieved to address the country's overwhelming problems of hunger and unemployment. Instead, Bosch appeared preoccupied with balance of payments deficits and extracting as much aid as possible from the US.

Yet while the US ambassador, John Bartlow Martin, himself criticised Bosch's inaction, the Dominican elite and the military suspected the PRD of tolerating and even collaborating with communists. Bosch always insisted that he was a radical nationalist and that the PRD had no sympathy for communism. Nevertheless, the pressure mounted against the PRD government, with 'Christian demonstrations', a damaging confrontation with 'Papa Doc' Duvalier of neighbouring Haiti and rising popular impatience. At a certain point, too, the US government clearly lost patience with Bosch, whose nationalism was easily interpreted as a threat to US economic and strategic interests. This view of events was supported by US ambassador Martin who questioned the role of communists in the government and who described the president as 'arrogant, vain, erratic' (Martin 1966:269).

Juan Bosch

'Juan Bosch was arrogant and vain. He sought not friends, but followers. He was not the leader of a modern political party, but a *caudillo*. He was an excellent novelist, but not a political theorist, nor, indeed, a towering figure of Latin American politics. But this *caudillo* wanted social change, this arrogant man believed in political democracy and, above all, he was scrupulously honest with public money. He loved his country and his countrymen — as children, perhaps, rather than brothers, but even this represented a drastic change in Dominican political life.

Bosch was not overthrown because he was arrogant and vain. Nor was he overthrown because of mistakes he made during his short administration. He was doomed from the start because his message and his promises were directed to the masses, the powerless *infelices*. His qualities, not his mistakes, led to his downfall. His search for social reforms and honest government arrayed against him the *gente de primera* [upper crust], already exasperated by their electoral defeat at the hand of a *de segunda* [commoner]. His nationalism and particularly his deep belief in political democracy cost him the support of the Kennedy administration. The Americans were unable to accept real, rather than formal Dominican independence. Above all, they wanted Bosch to persecute the 'Castro-Communists'. He refused. This was a mortal sin.'

(Gleijeses 1978:285)

Against a background of deteriorating economic conditions, the Dominican army overthrew Bosch in September 1963 and exiled him to Puerto Rico. The 'unfinished experiment', as Bosch called it, had lasted only seven months.

With Bosch's overthrow and the disarray of the PRD, the post-Trujillo power vacuum reappeared. The military installed a civilian *junta*, but unprecedented corruption and repression fuelled popular opposition. A series of plots, from left and right, were directed against the *junta*, and particularly Donald Reid Cabral, a prominent member of the oligarchy. Even with US$100 million in support (President Johnson had renewed links with the Dominican Republic after Kennedy's assassination in November 1963, ending a symbolic show of disapproval at the anti-Bosch coup), the *junta* barely survived until the spring of 1965. A condition of US support had been fresh elections that summer; Reid Cabral realised, however, that Bosch would probably win and announced that the country was not yet ready for further elections.

Reid Cabral's attempt to cling to power precipitated two simultaneous coups. One was led by the right-wing General Elias

US troops pass anti-American graffiti in Santo Domingo, 1965.
(Bernard Diederich)

Wessín y Wessín, who had led the overthrow of Bosch 19 months earlier and who now suspected Reid Cabral of wanting to take control of the military and its lucrative network of corruption. The other was the work of young army colonels associated with the underground PRD opposition who planned to reinstall Bosch as constitutionally elected president. Reid Cabral disappeared to Miami, while the two opposing army factions confronted one another. The pro-Bosch 'constitutionalists', however, had the people of Santo Domingo on their side. As the news of Reid Cabral's departure became known, a young PRD militant, José Francisco Peña Gómez urged the people onto the streets in a radio broadcast. A provisional government was established in the capital, awaiting the return of Bosch.

The right-wing 'loyalists', meanwhile, were horrified that the anti-Reid Cabral coup appeared to have become a popular uprising. From the San Isidro military base, General Wessín y Wessín ordered the bombing of the National Palace and other constitutionalist strongholds. In response, the constitutionalists, led by the charismatic Colonel Francisco Caamaño Deñó, distributed weapons to civilians and repulsed a tank attack. After a series of setbacks, the constitutionalists began to take control of the city, pushing back the loyalists who were working in direct collaboration with the US embassy and military attachés (Moreno 1970:29). The prospect of victory for the pro-Bosch forces brought a swift reaction from Washington. On 28 April 1965, the day after the constitutionalists took control of Santo Domingo, the first US troops landed. Within 48 hours, 23,000 US military personnel had arrived to join them. On 28 April President Johnson had given his reasons for the invasion: US citizens were at risk from the conflict. On 2 May, however, the more pressing US motives were revealed as President Johnson declared that 'what began as a popular democratic revolution... very shortly moved and was taken over and really seized and placed into the hands of a band of communist conspirators'. Protesting their neutrality, the US troops in fact sided directly with the loyalists and neutralised the constitutionalist force. Under the cover of a peace-keeping force from the Organisation of American States, the US occupation effectively defused the pro-Bosch movement, installing another friendly interim government and preparing the way for 'demonstration elections'.

The Dominican invasion was essentially a cold war exercise. 'What can we do in Vietnam', President Johnson is reported to have asked in April 1965, 'if we can't clean up the Dominican Republic?'(Martin 1966:661) In order to justify the exercise, a list of 58 alleged communists involved in the constitutionalist forces was released by the US authorities; many of these, journalists discovered, were dead, out of the country or simply innocent of the charge. Nonetheless, the State Department remained adamant that it had acted to forestall a communist takeover and civil war.

Balaguer: Repression and the 'Economic Miracle'

Joaquín Balaguer, supported by the US and the Dominican elite, won the June 1966 election by almost the same margin as Bosch had won in 1962. Bosch ran a subdued campaign; nonetheless, his bodyguard was murdered, his son shot, and hundreds of supporters assassinated, beaten and intimidated. Conducted under effective US military occupation, the election was deeply flawed and clearly biased in its operation in favour of Balaguer. Through fear and disillusionment, thousands of PRD followers abstained, while an overwhelming military presence at polling stations ensured that Dominicans voted in line with the army's instructions (Herman and Brodhead 1984:49).

The repression of the PRD and its supporters continued unabated after the inauguration of the Balaguer regime. A paramilitary death squad known as *la Banda* terrorised the slums of Santo Domingo in the late 1960s and early 1970s. In 1970, Amnesty International reported that a political murder victim was found in the streets of Santo Domingo every 34 hours. Between Balaguer's election in 1966 and the end of 1971 over 1,000 political assassinations took place in the

Dominican Republic, the overwhelming majority of victims coming from the PRD.

Little of this was reported in the US media. The Johnson administration, proud of its role in preventing Bosch's return to power, wholeheartedly supported the Balaguer government. US aid flowed into the Dominican Republic at a record rate; in 1966 economic and military assistance totalled US$111.16 million, the highest per capita US aid programme in the world excluding Vietnam. At that time, the US embassy in Santo Domingo employed 900 personnel (the biggest embassy in Latin America after Brazil). Of these, about 70 were involved in the Military Aid and Advisory Group (MAAG) which restructured and trained the Dominican military. Several of the high-ranking Dominican officers trained in anti-terrorist tactics in Texas were allegedly in charge of la Banda (Maríñez 1988:366).

The period which witnessed the systematic repression of former constitutionalists and PRD supporters was also that of the much-vaunted 'Dominican economic miracle'. Between 1969 and 1974 the country's Gross Domestic Product grew at an annual average of 11 per cent, one of the highest growth rates in the world. Due in part to massive US aid and foreign lending, the economic boom was also the result of high world prices for sugar, coffee, gold and other exports. The Balaguer regime also tore down many of the protectionist barriers set up under Trujillo and lured foreign investors with the promise of tax incentives and cheap labour. Thus began the Dominican Republic's diversification into tourism and Industrial Free Zones (see chapter 4). This combination of foreign capital, heavy borrowing, US largesse and high commodity prices financed Balaguer's lavish programme of public works. The broad avenues such as the 27 de Febrero and the tower blocks and civic buildings of modern Santo Domingo date from this period. It also paid for the import substitution policy which Balaguer pursued in the 1970s, encouraging local industry, private and state-run, to begin manufacturing goods for local consumption.

By 1974 the boom was over, and the oil crisis and recession of that year marked the beginning of economic crisis, worsened by the second worldwide oil shock of 1979, which has continued more or less unabated to the present day. The poorest sectors of Dominican society, moreover, had received little from the 'miracle'. Real wages were forcibly held down during the period, while inflation eroded poor families' purchasing power. The Balaguer regime's policies favoured foreign investors, agro-exporters and urban professionals at the expense of small farmers and rural communities. Bosch's 1963 constitution had limited foreign control of Dominican assets, prohibited large landholdings and provided for profit-sharing in agriculture and industry; Balaguer's 1966 constitution reversed all such measures, opening Dominican industry and agriculture to foreign investment. Poverty grew alarmingly in the countryside as land ownership became more concentrated (Georges 1990:34), leading to an upsurge in migration to Santo Domingo and abroad.

Limits of Democracy

With the country's most important political party dismantled and intimidated, Balaguer was able to win three consecutive elections, ruling until 1978. The PRD boycotted municipal elections in 1968 and refused to participate in the presidential election of May 1970. Amidst high levels of violence and repression (the PRD's radio broadcasts were censored) Balaguer won a second consecutive term of office with 55.7 per cent of the vote, beating a former political associate and vice-president, Francisco Augusto Lora.

By 1972 it had become apparent that Balaguer intended to stand again for the presidency. The following year, his hand was strengthened by an attempted guerrilla campaign, led by Colonel Caamaño who had mysteriously disappeared in 1967. Accompanied by ten men, Caamaño landed in February 1973 from Cuba and took to the mountains near Azua. Two weeks later the guerrillas were discovered and most of them killed by Dominican troops. In the meantime, Balaguer used the incident as a pretext to attack all opposition organisations which, he claimed, were plotting a combined insurrection and general strike. The president declared a state of emergency, sending in troops to shut down radio, newspaper and television offices, arrest over 1,400 union, student and political activists and patrol slum areas. Balaguer's political fortunes improved further that same year with the internal collapse of the PRD. Arguing in favour of renewed abstention from elections and proposing what he called 'dictatorship with popular support', Juan Bosch lost control of the PRD leadership and left to form the Dominican Liberation Party (PLD).

With the PRD in disarray and again boycotting elections, Balaguer won unopposed in May 1974. Only half of the two million Dominican voters participated. According to Jan Knippers Black, Balaguer and his Reformist Party (PR) took few chances in the run-up to the election:

> It soon became very clear, however, that Balaguer would brook no serious opposition. The armed forces were openly intimidating political leaders and would-be voters. Barracks throughout the country looked like PR headquarters, and soldiers carried PR flags at the ends of their bayonets. Although there is no evidence that Balaguer was aware of it, some military officers even conspired, as the elections approached, to assassinate [PRD leader] Peña Gómez. (1986:51)

Balaguer and the Military

Balaguer was a creation of the Trujillo period. His authoritarianism, while clearly less absolute and ruthless than Trujillo's, nevertheless depended on a similar relationship with the military. In the aftermath of the 1965 US invasion, his regime purged the armed forces of constitutionalists and rewarded those who had fought against Bosch's reinstatement. The government increased the military's budget, secretly transferring funds from health and education budgets, and appointed and promoted Balaguer loyalists. In his third Cabinet (1974-8) the president included three senior officers. Corruption became institutionalised as officers were given jobs in state enterprises and agencies:

> With few professional incentives or motivations, personal interests were paramount and led to corruption down to the lowest officer level. Officers were involved in enterprises of all kinds: large sugar plantations, hotel and casino ownership, ownership of communications media, light manufacturing, service stations, and a variety of small businesses. Most of Balaguer's generals were able to become multimillionaires through enterprises financed with government resources and through outright graft. (Pope Atkins 1981:52)

In return for a free hand in corruption and protected privileges, the 20,000-strong armed forces openly supported Balaguer and the PR, threatening opponents and participating in *la Banda*'s terrorist activities. Balaguer encouraged a cult of personality; troops referred to him as *el jefe* and posters with slogans such as 'Balaguer is My North Star' adorned every military and naval installation.

Using 'divide-and-rule' tactics, Balaguer was able to prevent any one military faction from becoming a threat. When the experienced coup-monger, General Wessín y Wessín, was revealed to be plotting against Balaguer in 1971, he was exiled to Spain, having first been publicly humiliated by Balaguer on a live television transmission. Other high-ranking officers were routinely transferred in order to prevent them from building up local power bases, while rival sections of the military were set against one another to strengthen presidential control over the armed forces as a whole.

Transition — With Conditions

By 1978, the Balaguer regime had become deeply unpopular. Economic recession, widespread corruption and authoritarian government replaced the brief euphoria of the 'miracle'. Worse still for Balaguer, the Carter administration in the US was taking a firm line on human rights and democratic practices, tying its economic aid to proven reforms in these fields. It became clear as elections once again approached that intimidation, cheating and an opposition boycott would jeopardise Dominican-US relations. In a cosmetic move, Balaguer allowed the Dominican Communist Party (PCD) to participate and invited election observers from the Organisation of American States. The PRD, having boycotted the two previous presidential contests, had meanwhile nominated as its own candidate Antonio Guzmán, formerly agriculture minister in the brief Bosch regime and a wealthy land-owner.

On election day, there were few reported incidents. Yet, as the results came in and it became plain that the PRD was winning, the military, with Balaguer's connivance, intervened. Occupying the offices of the JCE and taking over radio and television stations, the army denied that a coup was taking place but halted the public vote counting. The OAS and Carter administration reacted strongly; the US threatened an aid embargo, while Venezuela hinted strongly that it would cut off its supplies of oil to the Dominican Republic. Forced to make concessions by the strength of foreign and domestic opinion — Church, business and professional organisations all protested openly — Balaguer ordered the troops out of the JCE office, but condemned foreign interference and what he claimed was PRD-inspired electoral fraud. Finally, three weeks after the election, the results were announced: Guzmán 52 per cent; Balaguer 42 per cent; Bosch one per cent.

But although Balaguer had no choice but to concede defeat in the presidential contest, he managed to restrict the incoming PRD government's power by a number of strategies. Jerrymandering deprived the PRD of four senators and a seat in the chamber of deputies, allowing the *Reformistas* to keep their majority in the Senate and block legislation. An extraordinary session of the PR-dominated chamber of deputies voted large wage increases to the military and reduced civilian control over the security forces — days before the PRD government took over.

With its room for manoeuvre drastically reduced, the PRD government proceeded cautiously. Memories of the anti-Bosch coup remained strong, and Guzmán was in any case a conservative, disinclined to upset the Dominican elite. The PRD had also discarded much of the populism associated with Bosch and now presented itself as a technocratic and competent 'party of government'. Peña Gómez, the PRD leader most associated with the party's radical wing, left the country, ostensibly on extended travel leave. Before leaving, he warned: 'we are going into government, but we don't have power.

And without the force to back our actions it will be impossible to carry out changes.'

Yet, despite the restrictions imposed on it, the Guzmán regime was able to make important reforms in the military structure. Taking advantage of a large US delegation at his inauguration, the new president unexpectedly announced the retirement of Major General Neit Nivar Seijas, head of the powerful First Brigade and a Balaguer protegé, the secretary of the armed forces and the head of the navy. Within two years, Guzmán succeeded in retiring 600 officers, including 80 who had been in the highest echelons under Balaguer. Only one attempted coup, engineered in October 1979 by dismissed officers and some civilian PR supporters, created a short-lived alarm. The 'democratic opening' also encouraged a brief resurgence of trade union and popular organisation, similar to that which had occurred during Bosch's presidency.

Even more than with Bosch, however, the Guzmán government failed to deliver concrete reforms to the people who had voted it into power. Instead, presiding over a rapid economic decline, Guzmán tried to defuse popular unrest, impose austerity measures (mitigated by subsidies on basic goods and services) and attract further foreign investment and loans. His policies quickly alienated the PRD cadres and supporters, driving a deep rift between government and party. Guzmán, it seemed, had abandoned the PRD's platform of gradual reform in favour of an open alliance with those industrialists and investors who rejected Balaguer's dictatorial and centralised style of government. Reluctantly handing over the PRD presidential candidacy to Salvador Jorge Blanco, Guzmán ended his term highly unpopular and increasingly under pressure. In July 1982 he committed suicide, apparently worried that a vast corruption scandal involving close relatives was about to come into the open.

Against all predictions, meanwhile, the PRD had won a second term of office in May 1982. Jorge Blanco received 46 per cent of the vote, Balaguer 36 per cent and Bosch 10 per cent. The result was in part due to Balaguer's continuing unpopularity and the crisis within his party which led him to repudiate his own vice-presidential running-mate. It also revealed that Guzmán's personal unpopularity had not been transferred to the PRD, which presented its candidate, Jorge Blanco, as a man of honesty and liberal convictions.

Balaguer's Return

The second PRD government proved to be more corrupt, inefficient and repressive than its predecessor. The measures it took, under International Monetary Fund guidance, to correct the country's indebtedness led to near civil war and hundreds of deaths in April 1984 (see chapter 6). In terms of repression and military violence, the Jorge Blanco regime could claim little improvement on Balaguer's dubious record. Arbitrary arrests, police surveillance and paramilitary intimidation of trade unionists were commonplace.

Split by personal ambition and sectarianism, the PRD disintegrated during the Jorge Blanco administration. An open confrontation between Peña Gómez and Jacobo Majluta, Guzmán's vice-president, degenerated into violence in November 1985 when rival supporters fought among themselves at the party conference. Violence also marred the electoral campaign of 1986, as clashes between PRD activists and Balaguer supporters left several people dead. By this time, Peña Gómez had withdrawn from the PRD ticket, refusing to run as Majluta's vice-presidential candidate. The PRD therefore lost its most popular leader in addition to being thoroughly discredited after eight years of corruption and economic mismanagement.

Capitalising on the PRD's crisis, Balaguer won his fifth term in the May 16 elections, taking 41.6 per cent of the vote. Majluta received only 39.5 per cent, while Juan Bosch raised his percentage share from ten to 18.4. The usual allegations of fraud abounded. Vote counting was stopped in the week following polling after Majluta had challenged the process and called on the JCE to resign. After the presidential result was confirmed, the JCE took controversial decisions over who had won senatorial and mayoral elections in Santo Domingo. The outcome was a violent PRD demonstration and shoot-out in front of the JCE office in which four people were killed by police.

Ushered into power by the collapse of the PRD, the new Balaguer regime was soon in conflict, not with the established political parties but with a growing and militant popular movement (See chapter 6). After a period of relative stability, a wave of strikes began in February 1988, demanding wage increases, protesting at high prices and calling for better public services. Balaguer responded with customary ruthlessness; by early March, ten protestors had been killed, 20 wounded and thousands arrested. Speaking of the high incidence of violent incidents involving the security forces, the president blamed 'uncontrollable elements' within the police and military. The repression of anti-government protest continued unabated through 1988; in November, former president Majluta warned that Dominican democracy was in 'grave danger'. A popular explosion, he predicted, could result in a military dictatorship, 'worse than Pinochet's and without its economic competence.'

The authoritarian response to popular demands was coupled with occasional conciliatory gestures designed to defuse tension. Public-sector wage rises and the freezing of food prices were announced in mid-March 1988 as the government negotiated with business leaders, trade unions and a delegation from the Church. Characteristically, the representatives from the popular movements were excluded from the talks.

By the middle of his fifth term of office, it had become apparent that Balaguer intended to stand for a sixth. Despite divisions within his own party, a rapidly deteriorating economy and widespread unpopularity, Balaguer was reportedly determined to be in office and to preside over the official celebrations for the 500th anniversary of Columbus' arrival in Hispaniola. The massive programme of construction connected with the anniversary had created an estimated 30,000 jobs which the president hoped would translate into votes. He also recognised that the continuing crisis inside the PRD and the rise of Bosch's PLD could well split the opposition vote and give him power once more.

Transition or Facade?

That Joaquín Balaguer could successfully win the 1990 elections says much about his political acumen and stamina. It also reflects on the organisational and ideological weakness of the main opposition parties, which together polled almost 60 per cent of the vote, but which were unable to reach any tactical agreement to stop Balaguer. Instead, the PLD and the PRD, at loggerheads since the 1970s and dominated by personal ambitions and animosities, refused to cooperate. The PRD, for the first time in its history, was pushed into third place, while the PLD continued its spectacular rise, officially winning 34 per cent of the votes, and claiming a much higher percentage.

The election campaign was fought amidst continual references to the past. Balaguer's slogan, 'un camino sin peligro' ('a safe path') was part of a propaganda offensive against both Bosch and Peña Gómez, whom he explicitly linked to the instability and civil conflict of the 1960s. Bosch's old adversaries, the Church hierarchy and the military, again accused the former president of atheism and anti-army sentiments. The issue of Peña Gómez's parentage also resurfaced, with the familiar allegations that his family background (and by implication his loyalties) lay in Haiti rather than the Dominican Republic. As in previous elections, the campaign was dominated by personal attacks rather than real policy debate.

The allegations of electoral fraud and corruption reinforced doubts over the real extent of the much-vaunted transition to democracy since Trujillo. Not only was the election discredited by the widespread accusations of malpractice, but the massive scale of popular abstention revealed a continuing lack of confidence in the process among large numbers of Dominicans. As a result, the 1990 Balaguer regime took office with the electoral support of only 18 per cent of Dominican voters. The readiness of powerful groups, such as the armed forces and the Church, to intervene in the political debates also raised questions about the level of democracy in the country. Many Dominicans even doubted whether the military would have permitted Juan Bosch to assume the presidency if the result had favoured the PLD.

Political analysts have pointed to the democratic progress made by the Dominican Republic since Trujillo's death in 1961. In particular, they refer to the multi-party system, the regular four-yearly elections and the transfer of power from Balaguer to the PRD in 1978 and vice-versa in 1986 as proof of a change in political concepts and practices. Noting these developments, Christian Girault (1988:50) writes:

> In less than a decade, the Dominican Republic has taken important steps towards establishing a truly representative democracy. The country seems — at last — to be emerging from the vicious circle of dictatorships and military coups which have characterised its political life since independence.

While it is true that the military has abstained from direct intervention since 1982, it would be difficult to argue that the Dominican Republic enjoys a 'representative democracy'. Instead, the limited democratic opening represented by the PRD governments of 1978-86 has largely disappeared, with a return to the authoritarian rule of Balaguer.

Certain advances in democratic and human rights since 1961 are undeniable. A relatively free press functions, and open discussion of political questions is now taken for granted. For generations of Dominicans used to the stifling and pervasive presence of Trujillo and his secret agents the modern-day Dominican Republic appears liberal and unrepressive in comparison. Perhaps most importantly, there is now a distinction between 'political' and 'private' life. The long hand of el jefe no longer reaches into every corner of existence.

The military has also been removed from the centre stage of Dominican politics, even though the armed forces remain numerically strong for a country which has fought no foreign wars since 1865. The army numbers 15,000, the navy 4,000 and the airforce 3,800; there are also an estimated 1,000 paramilitary police. After President Guzmán's purge of the top military echelons the army has been reluctant to become politically involved, yet it is frequently used for the repression of popular unrest. It continues to attract recruits from poor rural backgrounds, and the officer class shows little of the elitism characteristic of other Latin American militaries.

Yet despite such improvements, real democratic reform in terms of power and participation has yet to materialise. On one level, the constitutional processes of democratic government appear to take place; on another, the party political system works according to its own rules of corruption and personal power, from which the great majority of people are excluded. In the view of Catherine M. Conaghan and Rosario Espinal (1990:572):

> More than a decade has passed since the Dominican Republic underwent its transition to democracy, but 'normality' has not yet become a feature of political life. Electoral rotation has been achieved, but periodic interruptions of democratic procedures and practices still occur, especially in institutional conflict-resolution and decision-making. Behind the facade of democratic politics, a shadow world of extra-institutional and extra-legal manoeuvring remains.

In the latter part of 1991, the prospects for 'normality' in the Dominican Republic seemed more remote than ever. Revealingly, in April 1991, the US company, Political Risk Services, identified the Dominican Republic and Peru as the two Latin American countries with the highest risk of political and civil turmoil over the next five-year period.

Thirty years after the fall of Trujillo, Dominican political life was still dominated by those who had lived through, and even worked for, the dictatorship. To a large extent, hopes for real change had been frustrated by military force, US intervention, fraudulent elections and the weaknesses of the political establishment. 'One reasonable conclusion about Dominican politics', observe Kryzanek and Wiarda (1988:87), 'is that nothing — no political regime — has worked well.'

In the face of a chronic economic decline, widespread disillusionment and social conflict, such pessimism seems justified. A victim of internal and external pressures, the PRD squandered its opportunity to offer the Dominican people an alternative to Balaguer's authoritarian rule. The survival of the *caudillo* tradition has also impeded democratic change, maintaining a fossilised system of personality politics which looks back to the 1960s for its inspiration. 'Democratic consolidation in the Dominican Republic', writes Jonathan Hartlyn (1991:206), 'is difficult to conceive without significant socioeconomic changes towards a more vigorous and participatory society'. As the current political establishment offers few prospects of such changes, Dominicans are increasingly turning to other forms of participation.

3

Power and Glory

In the suburban sprawl of eastern Santo Domingo, a vast cross-shaped concrete monument — 800 feet long, 150 feet tall — has risen into the city's skyline. The *faro a Colón* or Columbus lighthouse is the Dominican Republic's commemorative tribute to the explorer's arrival in Hispaniola on 12 October 1492. The Ministry of Tourism promotes the country as 'the land Columbus loved best'; the government intends to attract millions of tourists during the 1992 quincentenary and afterwards with the lighthouse and a programme of celebratory events. The huge monument, started and abandoned during the Trujillo regime, is to hold Columbus's mortal remains and to project a crucifix of light miles into the sky above Santo Domingo.

For many Dominicans, the *faro a Colón*, with its grandiose aspirations towards posterity, is seen as much as a monument to the personality of Joaquín Balaguer as to Columbus. Critics have judged its enormous cost, estimated at anywhere between US$40 million and US$250 million, as inappropriate and extravagant, and there is widespread indignation that Columbus's arrival, associated by many with colonial exploitation and indigenous genocide, should be celebrated at all. The whole programme of construction to beautify Santo Domingo has also caused bitter controversy. In order to build the lighthouse and surrounding buildings, the authorities evicted almost 2,000 families living in the existing slum area. According to Jorge Cela, a Jesuit priest campaigning for their rights, most were lucky to receive US$50 before seeing their shacks bulldozed. Other critics of the scheme estimate that as many as 100,000 people have been adversely affected by new construction work such as road building and slum clearance. They also claim that these slums have not been replaced by any alternative form of accommodation for the city's poorest people. The official version of events is different: ministers insist that each family is rehoused in

The Columbus lighthouse under construction, 1991.   (Julio Etchart)

the new apartment blocks which line the road from the airport to the city centre.

Balaguer's personal enthusiasm for the lighthouse and the 1992 celebrations has pushed the project through to completion despite concerted opposition from those affected by the 'beautification' programme. This says much about Balaguer's individual obsession with grand construction projects, but also reflects more generally on the concentration of executive power and resources in the hands of the president. According to the Dominican Centre of Education Studies (CEDEE), Balaguer personally controlled 53 per cent of the 1989 national budget. A fierce debate around the 1991 budget revealed that the government had manipulated ministerial allocations in order to increase Balaguer's personal budget. The presidency (Balaguer's department), the PLD opposition claimed, had spent 15 times more than its official allocation for 1990.

According to Article 4 of the Dominican constitution, 'the government of the nation is essentially civilian, republican, democratic and representative'. In practice, it is highly centralised and authoritarian, with overwhelming executive power belonging to the president, who can effectively rule by decree if necessary. Furthermore, the president is entitled to appoint and dismiss cabinet ministers and

The Messiah

'Every Saturday and Sunday, the president roams around the rural backwaters of the Dominican Republic. He arrives by helicopter and listens to the complaints of smallholders and landless *campesinos* who spontaneously and passionately air their grievances. When they have finished speaking into the microphone, they draw nearer to tell him their troubles, almost whispering into his ear as if in confession. They tell him about the overdue mortgage, the money they need for an operation, a sewing machine for the wife, a bicycle for a son, or a pregnant pig.

Balaguer grants their wishes with an immediate order or makes sure that they are given a pass to see him in the presidential palace in Santo Domingo. Then he begins to speak, publicly ridiculing his own ministers and administrators for their incompetence or berating some local landowner for monopolising the irrigation scheme and leaving no water for the smallholders, "with the complicity of the military" — who, standing by, listen impassively to the president's attack. The *campesinos* worship him like some sort of messiah. A women in the audience in the village of Las Guáranas suddenly falls into epileptic convulsions.'

José Comas, 'La Transformación del señor presidente'. *El País Internacional*, 1 June 1987.

all civil servants without reference to Congress, thereby giving the head of state almost unlimited powers of patronage.

I, The Supreme

The centralisation of power and finance has given Balaguer ample scope to play the traditional role of *caudillo*, dispensing money and services on personal whim rather than institutional priority. The president makes almost daily appearances at the inauguration of schools, clinics, roads and housing projects, where the beneficiaries are encouraged to show their gratitude — and political allegiance — to *el jefe*. Like Trujillo, Balaguer prides himself on his personal contact with individuals and communities, often travelling by helicopter to remote rural villages to attend inauguration ceremonies and other meetings.

The personalisation of political power in the Dominican Republic has tended to weaken both government institutions and political parties. Balaguer, for instance, has always received individual petitioners in the presidential palace, refusing to delegate responsibility to appropriate ministers or government agencies. His choice of ministers and political advisers has often been idiosyncratic, reflecting his private agenda more than any commitment to a party programme. Following his electoral victory in 1986, Balaguer made a series of bizarre cabinet appointments, aimed at coopting former adversaries and weakening opposition organisations. He gave the powerful post of Interior Minister to General Wessín y Wessín, whom he had exiled 15 years earlier on charges of plotting a coup. Equally unpredictable was his decision to appoint General Antonio Imbert Barrera as Secretary of Defence, since Imbert was the last surviving member of the group which assassinated Balaguer's erstwhile mentor, Trujillo. Wessín was subsequently to replace Imbert after a rumoured coup attempt in June that year, only to be dismissed again in June 1991. With another post going to Donald Reid Cabral (see p.27), Balaguer's cabinet resembled a roll-call of the main figures involved in the turbulent early 1960s.

The selection of ministers and advisers irrespective of party affiliation emphasises the importance of *personalismo* above conventional political criteria. The president appoints and dismisses according to what seem to be individual whims, while potential rivals within the party are consciously ignored or kept from accumulating too much power. Since founding the Reformist Party in 1963 (and renaming it the Social Christian Reformist Party in 1984), Balaguer has fended off several attempts from rivals inside the organisation to supercede him and has maintained his monopoly of party power. In the words of one academic commentator, the party is no more than a 'patronage and campaign organisation for the president' (Pope Atkins 1981:21).

It's My Party

Personal power, charisma and ambition have also dominated the other main Dominican parties. The PLD was from the outset the personal vehicle of Juan Bosch and is all but synonymous with its leader. It was established after Bosch found his personal political philosophy opposed by a majority in the PRD, leading him to form a breakaway party. Although there are other nationally recognised leaders in the PLD and a tendency towards factionalism, Bosch reigns supreme in his party. When, in March 1991, Bosch resigned from the leadership of the PLD it was for two weeks only. He withdrew his resignation, he claimed, because of overwhelming public pressure for him to stay in charge of the party.

In the case of the PRD, personalism has been even more controversial and destructive. Formed by Bosch and other exiled social democrats in 1939, the party contained conflicting political tendencies but was initially held together by Bosch's personality and by a unified opposition to the Trujillo dictatorship. Following the brief Bosch presidency, the 1963 coup and the US invasion, the PRD began to lose its sense of unity and purpose. During Balaguer's first extended period in power (1966-78), it entered into a period of introspection, during which Bosch rejected social democracy and called for 'dictatorship with popular support'. This concept was rebuffed by a social-democratic majority, led by Peña Gómez, resulting in Bosch's resignation.

Since Bosch's departure, Peña Gómez has been the single most influential PRD leader, but his political fortunes have been marred by continual allegations that his loyalties lie more with Haiti than with the Dominican Republic. Various would-be *caudillos* have fought for control of the party, competing for Peña Gómez's support and for the party's presidential nomination. The relatively short four-year presidential term in the Dominican Republic has meant that these factional struggles are an almost permanent feature of political life, as would-be candidates campaign for the next election.

The power struggle between Guzmán and Jorge Blanco in the 1970s and 1980s (see p.34) has been succeeded by a bitter rivalry into the 1990s between Peña Gómez and Jacobo Majluta. So divided was the PRD during the Guzmán regime of 1978-82, for instance, that its senators sided with PR opponents to block presidential programmes of legislation. The acrimony surrounding the PRD presidential nomination for the 1986 election was even worse; in December 1985 armed supporters of Peña Gómez seized the party's national headquarters following violent clashes at the PRD conference in which two activists were killed. Peña Gómez later refused to stand as Majluta's vice-presidential running-mate, Majluta having already turned his faction, *La Estructura* (the structure), into an entirely separate electoral campaign vehicle. By the 1990 elections, the division had widened still further. With Peña Gómez standing for the first time as official PRD candidate, Majluta formed the breakaway Independent Revolutionary Party (PRI). Taking almost seven per cent of the votes, Majluta effectively split the PRD's support, reducing Peña Gómez's share to 23 per cent.

The fierce rivalries between individuals and factions within Dominican political parties have caused numerous splits, regroupings and alliances. This has been particularly the case with those party and trade union organisations on the left, which since 1978 have been involved in a continual process of disintegration. According to Vanna

Ianni (1987:120), no fewer than 42 left-wing groups appeared between 1978 and 1986 during the more liberal PRD period, many surviving hardly a year before splitting again. In the absence of stable party structures, politicians have resorted to political horse-trading, sacrificing ideological considerations for immediate electoral gain. In Dominican elections, smaller parties usually pledge their votes to one of the major candidates, in return for promises of favours and appointments. In this system, the far-right Quisqueyan Democratic Party (PQD), led by veteran conspirator General Wessín y Wessín, gave its 1.21 per cent of the 1990 presidential vote to Balaguer, ensuring his slight lead over Bosch. Equally, the far-left Socialist Bloc (BS) and a section of the Dominican Workers' Party (PTD) each provided Peña Gómez with 0.14 per cent of the vote, both receiving a seat in the chamber of deputies in return.

The Dominican political process occasionally produces strange bed fellows. In 1972, for instance, the so-called Santiago Accord brought together three parties in a common front against Balaguer. The parties were the PRD, an ephemeral grouping known as the MIDA and Wessín's PQD. That only nine years earlier, Wessín had forcibly overthrown Bosch's PRD administration says much about the opportunism of Dominican party politics. Conversely, the deliberate rejection by Bosch of any electoral alliance with Peña Gómez in 1990 was seen by many Dominicans as proof that Bosch was happier with a Balaguer victory than with sharing government with his former colleagues and now his bitter adversaries in the PRD.

Clientilism

Despite the concentration of political power in individual hands, party politics in the Dominican Republic arouse deep passions. Fights and killings between rival party activists, and supporters of different factions within parties, have been commonplace since the 1960s. During election campaigns the entire country is highly politicised and tense, with huge meetings, cavalcades and a constant barrage of party propaganda. Travelling through the Dominican countryside, it is difficult to find a single wall, tree or lamppost that is not adorned with the name and colours of a political party. The electioneering style owes much to the US model, concentrating on personalities at the expense of policy debate. Dirty tricks are also a common tactic, aimed at undermining the credibility of presidential candidates. In the 1990 election campaign, for instance, a fax purporting to originate from a Cuban hospital was circulated among the media. It claimed to show that Juan Bosch was suffering from Alzheimer's Disease, and was later reported to have been forged by *Reformista* supporters.

The intense loyalty which Dominican parties inspire and the lengths that they will go to in order to win power are primarily a result of the relationship between political office and economic advancement. The Dominican political system has been described as a 'winner takes all' arrangement, in which the huge power invested in the presidency is hardly counterbalanced by the legislature. During Balaguer's tenure of office, moreover, the Chamber of Deputies and Senate have usually contained a *Reformista* majority, thus giving the President a free hand to introduce measures without effective opposition. As a result, taking the presidency means taking control of the state budget and distributing resources accordingly.

The 'spoils system' connected to political power is particularly important in the Dominican Republic, since the government directly controls a large proportion of the economy. This is a direct legacy of the Trujillo years, when the dictatorship centralised economic control on a personal basis. Upon the assassination of Trujillo, these assets passed into state ownership. They include the State Sugar Council (CEA); the Dominican Electricity Corporation (CDE); the Dominican State Corporation (CORDE); and the Institute for Price Stabilisation (INESPRE). These large organisations administrate the all-important sugar industry, electricity generation, several key industries (cement, brewing, insurance) and food prices. The state also runs its own airline, transport network and large areas of land.

The Dominican state sector regularly loses money and costs the government dear in subsidies and public debt. According to the Inter-American Development Bank: 'Overall public-sector deficits averaged six per cent of GDP in the period 1986-89, and this, because of the limited availability of external financing, became the major source of monetary expansion, rapid inflation, foreign-exchange outflows and exchange rate instability' (IADB 1990:95). But these 'corrupt, patronage-bloated, ailing and inefficient public enterprises' (Kryzanek and Wiarda 1988:132) are important tools in the system of incentives and rewards which makes up Dominican politics. Most importantly, they provide jobs. Perhaps as many as 300,000 Dominicans are employed in state-owned enterprises, representing ten per cent of the national labour force. Overmanning is just one aspect of the state sector which has a well justified reputation for extraordinary inefficiency. The CDE, in particular, incites scorn and anger among all Dominicans for its failure to provide a rudimentary electricity supply.

To a certain extent, all state-sector jobs are political appointments. From high-ranking public functionaries to office cleaners, government

Power Failure

Bars, cinemas and restaurants in Santo Domingo normally advertise their attractions with the phrase *hay planta* ('we've got a generator'). The streets of the colonial quarter are littered with humming, smoking generators, powering shops, offices and private homes. Every hotel has its own power supply. Meanwhile, most people in the capital city are lucky to receive four hours a day of electricity. In the countryside it is worse. Often power cuts last for days.

Under the CDE, founded in 1955, generating capacity in the Dominican Republic has actually fallen by 50 per cent since the mid-1980s. As a result, the national system is believed to meet only one half of the economy's needs. Companies often choose to opt out of the national grid altogether and to install their own generating capacity. Most Dominicans do not have this choice and are unable to use refrigerators, cookers or lights. Hospitals have to depend on their own oil-powered generators.

The government blames the price of imported oil (obtained at preferential rates from Venezuela and Mexico) for the power shortages. It also concedes that power stations are outdated and inefficient. According to the CDE, many Dominicans fail to pay their electricity bills and illegal tapping into the mains supply is widespread. Yet, when necessary, the power supply can improve. During the last days of the 1990 election campaign, for instance, power cuts all but ceased in what appeared to be a crude political gesture by the Balaguer government.

Balaguer has spoken of privatising the ailing CDE and bringing in foreign management as a solution to the problem, yet few foreign investors would be interested in such a rundown industry. As a concession to public opinion, the president sacked the head of the CDE, Ramón Pérez Mártinez, in August 1991, after the latter had fired 3,000 workers but failed to make any improvement in the power supply. Pérez Mártinez was the sixth head of the CDE to be dismissed by Balaguer since 1986.

employees are expected to show allegiance to the ruling party and president. A change of government is therefore a catastrophic prospect for those already in public-sector posts and an alluring proposition for those with loyalties to the next ruling party. An incoming government will inevitably purge prominent opposition supporters, replacing them with its own loyalists. Political support will also be rewarded by privileged access to a range of services and opportunities. In the small coastal town of Paraiso, for instance, a modern housing complex stands out from the older, ramshackle buildings. Each apartment has a cock emblazoned on the wall by the front door. This signifies allegiance to

Balaguer's party and hints none too subtly at the criteria underlying the choice of tenants.

An organisation such as INESPRE, ostensibly established to act as honest intermediary between peasant producer and urban consumer, also offers ample opportunities for political manipulation. The agency buys sugar from the state-owned industry, holds a monopoly on certain imports such as cooking oil and is generally intended to hold down the price of such staples as rice by controlling their distribution. However, the so-called *ventas populares* (popular sales), which may involve unloading food from a lorry in a slum area, are frequently politically motivated and often correspond to visits from politicians and electoral campaign meetings.

Corruption

In the modern sector of Santo Domingo one multi-storey building stands higher and more imposingly than the others. It houses the myriad government departments and agencies which make up the Dominican state bureaucracy. The building is universally known as the *huacal* (the crate), and at first it seems that the nickname reflects its appearance. But in Dominican slang, a *botella* (a bottle) is a job offering opportunities for bribes and corruption. It is therefore logical that those holding the *botellas* should work inside the *huacal*.

The name given to the government offices underlines the widespread acceptance of official corruption in the Dominican system. As Ian Bell remarks (1981:207), 'any administrative machine powered by low-grade fuels in the shape of underpaid officials requires a certain amount of palm-greasing as a lubricant to keep the wheels turning'. Corruption takes many forms, from petty abuses of power to multi-million dollar frauds. Badly paid policemen, for example, harass street vendors or stop motorists and accuse them of speeding. A small bribe is the accepted way of winning a temporary reprieve from the much more expensive business of losing a driving licence or going to court. At the other extreme, the managers of large state-owned enterprises are always vulnerable to tempting financial offers from businesses and other government departments.

During the Trujillo period, the dictator personally ran all aspects of the economy and government, permitting limited corruption among his clique of supporters but maintaining absolute control of lucrative sources of revenue. In the aftermath of the dictatorship, competing interest groups tried to take over Trujillo's former interests. The brief Bosch presidency marked an exceptional period of reform, during which he strongly discouraged corruption and largely cleaned up the public sector. But when Bosch was overthrown in the 1963 coup, institutional corruption returned with a vengeance:

As if trying to make up for the seven months lost during his administration, government servants engaged in a rash of corrupt practices... Bribes to administration officials, for example, occurred on a scale almost matching that of the [Trujillo] era. Government offices became so overstaffed that many were receiving salaries without rendering any services. More importantly, the spirit of fraud which characterized every aspect of government under the slain Generalissimo again was rampant in the public service — the enrichment of favored individuals through the expenditure of funds for public projects, self-aggrandizement through one's knowledge of pending government programs, the receipt of goods, favor or money through the performance of an official duty. (Gleijeses 1978:116)

At the same time, Balaguer imposed harsh austerity measures, holding down public-sector wages while allowing prices to rise. By the end of 1977 a government salary was worth less than half its 1970 value. The exaction of 'speed payments' and the holding of two or more parallel 'jobs' therefore became a survival response to government policy on the part of the beleaguered middle class.

Each succeeding regime has accused its predecessor of corruption on an unprecedented scale. The Balaguer regime of 1966-78 faced continual allegations of financial irregularities. According to NACLA *Report on the Americas* in 1982, the regime looked after its own:

Ultimately half of the national budget went directly to Balaguer's office, where he personally managed the reins of fiscal administration and patronage. He would give a contract to one friend for a six-mile section of the Duarte highway, award the Valdesia Dam to another, the national stadium to a third. The recipients of such contracts and favors were few: no more than six companies received 95% of the value of all public works during some years. (NACLA, vol XVI, no 6, p.11)

While even his most ardent opponents accept that Balaguer is innocent of personal self-enrichment, it is widely accepted that he has allowed individuals and groups — ministers, prominent businessmen, the military — to make illicit fortunes. The Air Force reputedly takes a cut from *narcotraficante* activity through the Dominican Republic, the Army controls the payments taken from Haitians illegally entering the country, and the Navy owns the concession on permitting clandestine emigration of Dominicans by boat to Puerto Rico. The boom in public works during the early 1990s has reinforced allegations that there is no proper competitive bidding for building contracts.

Several scandals in 1991 confirmed that corruption in high places continues unabated. Early that year, for instance, it was revealed that Tourism Minister Andrés Vanderhorst had approved the sale of a golf course near Puerto Plata to a German company at a quarter of its valuation price. The sale was eventually cancelled after accusations of financial impropriety. Suspicions also surrounded the government's contract with a Canadian company, Hydro-Québec, to renovate the Santo Domingo electricity supply when it was discovered that US$20 million of the government's deposit had been removed from a bank account. Subsequently, Rafael Bello Andino, Balaguer's personal advisor and de facto prime minister, was sacked.

The PRD governments of 1978-86 hardly fared better in terms of scandal and public disillusionment. During the Guzmán regime, the public-sector pay-roll increased by 72 per cent, and charges of corruption were levelled against several high-ranking officials, including vice-president Majluta who was also head of the state agency, CORDE. Guzmán's suicide in 1982 was widely put down to the impending revelation of massive corruption among his family circle.

The succeeding Jorge Blanco administration reached new levels of cronyism. Charges of embezzlement, drug trafficking and money laundering abounded. This was particularly ironic, since Jorge Blanco had made honesty and accountability central themes of his election campaign. In 1987, the year after Balaguer returned to power, Jorge Blanco was accused of misusing public funds and, together with his former defence minister and other officials, of accepting illegal commissions of US$3.5 million on purchases of military equipment. Pleading heart trouble, he escaped to the US via the Venezuelan embassy and a hospital, and was sentenced *in absentia* to a 20-year prison sentence. The country, said Balaguer, was in 'a state of putrefaction' under Jorge Blanco, yet several observers agreed that there was little to choose between the various recent governments. Only Juan Bosch escaped the charges of institutionalised corruption; his 1986 election slogan, 'neither a killer nor a thief', was a clear reference to Balaguer's human rights record and Jorge Blanco's controversial past financial dealings. In August 1991 Jorge Blanco's 20-year sentence was confirmed after a lengthy trial during which the former president, who had believed that he would prove his innocence, collapsed in court.

President Joaquín Balaguer inaugurates an irrigation system, San Cristóbal, 1991.

(Julio Etchart)

Politics of Pragmatism

Personality politics and widespread corruption tend to obscure the ideological differences between the main Dominican parties. Since the near-civil war of 1965 these differences have gradually diminished as the most important electoral organisations have adopted broadly similar political platforms, seeking to stress the strengths and weaknesses of individual politicians rather than radically alternative policies. Additionally, the reputations of key politicians remain largely determined by the events of the immediate post-Trujillo period, giving Dominican politics a backward-looking emphasis. Above all, however, Dominican politics operate on a much more pragmatic than ideological basis.

Of the three main parties Balaguer's Social Christian Reformist Party is the most traditionally conservative, stressing patriotism and Catholic values. Its electoral support comes mostly from the country's most backward rural areas, where Balaguer is widely revered for his land reform programme and other occasional clientilist largesse. The conservative hierarchy of the Catholic church, headed by the controversial Archbishop of Santo Domingo, Cardinal Nicolás Jesús López Rodríguez, openly supports Balaguer. The party also receives the financial backing of the post-Trujillo economic elite which has done well out of Balaguer's building boom and the growth of the new economic sectors. The PRSC claims the credit for the spectacular expansion of the Industrial Free Zones and tourism (see chapter 4) and harks nostalgically back to the 'miracle' years of the late 1960s and early 1970s.

The rival PRD also claims responsibility for diversifying the Dominican economy between 1978 and 1986. During its periods of government, including the ephemeral Bosch presidency, its rhetoric of nationalism and popular reform has given way to austerity policies virtually indistinguishable from those imposed by Balaguer. Less cohesive than the *Reformistas*, the PRD has been wracked by internal disputes, reflecting the political, as well as personal, differences between reformers such as Peña Gómez and conservatives such as Majluta. The party's 1990 election campaign contained progressive proposals on trade union and women's rights, and Peña Gómez adopted some of the populist tone of Bosch's 1962 campaign. Yet the PRD was chastened and discredited by its last term in office, when corruption and social disorder reached unprecedented levels. While it still appeals to sectors of the working class and peasantry, its real power base lies among the urban lower middle class.

Both the *Reformistas* and the PRD have established institutional links with international organisations. These links act as a conduit for funds

The Bosch Pendulum

'In 1982, the PLD was still somewhat of a leftist party, but by 1986 there was virtually no substantive difference between the platforms of the PRD and the PLD. And by the 1990 elections, the PLD's program was actually to the right of all the other major political parties, advocating economic privatization.

There is nothing leftist any more about the PLD's platform: Bosch has returned to his anticommunist populism, and his electoral program is really the most coherent plan for restructuring Dominican capitalism. If the upper class had any political sense, it would be behind Bosch, but he has only been accepted by a sophisticated sector of the elite.

The PLD continues to be a social democratic-style alternative, even without the theoretical philosophy of social democracy. Within the PLD, there are still many people who consider themselves leftists. Why do they work for the PLD, with a rightist program? Because they believe that at this moment there is nothing else to do. For one thing, they are faithful followers of Bosch. Bosch is a *caudillo* leader and they trust that what *el jefe* does is correct. Secondly, they are looking for a way to survive politically, to be able to form a democratic, reformist government: privatize, but then improve living conditions through state programs in education, health, housing and welfare. They see the PLD as an arena for social action.'

Roberto Cassá, interviewed by Robert Fox and Michael Kamber, NACLA *Report on the Americas*, vol.XXIV, no.3, 1990.

and other forms of support and are also a means of enhancing the parties' domestic image. The PRD is a member of the social-democratic Socialist International, and Peña Gómez has become a prominent spokesperson inside the International. The *Reformistas* took over the small Revolutionary Social Christian Party (PRSC) in 1984 and incorporated the Social Christian title into their name, thereby gaining access to the resources of the Christian Democrat International through a marriage of convenience.

Juan Bosch's PLD attracts the poorest social sectors, loyal to the memory of Bosch's erstwhile populism. But what populism there was became transformed by the early 1990s into allegiance to orthodox neo-liberal economic restructuring. In the 1990 election campaign, for instance, the PLD advocated widespread privatisation within the Dominican state sector, arguing for greater efficiency through competition. Not surprisingly, the PLD won support from several prominent industrialists and entrepreneurs, who saw the party as a better option for modernising the Dominican economy than the more traditional state sector-oriented opposition. According to eminent Dominican historian, Roberto Cassá, Bosch underwent a complete political transformation in the course of the 1980s, moving to the right of even his former antagonists.

The unspoken political — if not personal — consensus between the major parties and personalities was particularly conspicuous in June 1991, when Balaguer ordered the repatriation of all Haitians aged under 16 and over 60. Although the PLD urged that the repatriations be carried out humanely, Bosch fully supported Balaguer's decision, arguing that Haitian workers were responsible for low wages and high unemployment in the Dominican Republic. More generally, the three main parties compete for the approval of the US government, and criticism of US foreign policy or business interests inside the country is rare. During the 1990 election campaign, Bosch specifically emphasised his commitment to the free-market development model and praised the role of Puerto Rico as a regional example of successful free enterprise.

Apres Moi?

The personalities which have dominated politics in the Dominican Republic for 30 years cannot go on beyond the mid-1990s. Both Balaguer and Bosch have said that they may have to retire soon and early in 1992 Balaguer confirmed that he would not seek re-election. Whatever their decisions, there will be fierce battles for succession in both parties. Various contenders have already declared themselves, and it remains to be seen which would-be successor can best manipulate the machinery of each party. The competition for the leadership of the PRSC will be particularly fierce. By September 1991 four senior *Reformistas* had already announced that they would seek the party candidature for the next election. They included former vice-president, Fernando Alvarez Bogaert, Santo Domingo senator, Jacinto Peynado, and ex-head of the CDE, Ramón Pérez Martínez. The Dominican press, meanwhile, speculated that other, hitherto unannounced, candidates would include Vice-President Carlos Morales Troncoso, Central Bank Governor Luis Toral and the veteran conservative, Donald Reid Cabral. The formation of a faction within the PRSC calling itself 'Lo Que Balaguer Diga' ('Whatever Balaguer Says') confirmed beliefs that Vice-President Morales Troncoso would project himself as Balaguer's heir.

More important than the identity of these political heirs is whether the disappearance of Balaguer and Bosch will end the Dominican *caudillo* tradition. A generation of politicians raised on Balaguer's authoritarian practices and highly centralised government may well be inclined to continue in much the same way. So ingrained, too, is the system of patronage and clientilism that it would be impossible to dismantle it quickly. Yet there is also apprehension among Dominicans as to what will follow Balaguer's regime. If the PRSC and PLD disintegrate into warring factions there is every chance of increased social violence and instability.

But the reform of the Dominican political structure is seen by many as long overdue. Pressure groups, from right and left, are critical of the anachronistic and authoritarian style of Dominican governments. The National Renovation Movement (MODERNO), for instance, represents a younger, more dynamic generation of enterpreneurs than those who support the traditional parties. In a series of pamphlets, it has criticised what it sees as excessive centralism and abuses of state power. Its recipe for greater freedoms — economic and political — is the gradual dismantling of the monolithic Dominican state. A similarly radical, but politically opposed, challenge is issued by the popular movement and its myriad local organisations (see chapter 6). With the disappearance of the old patriarchs of Dominican politics, the challenges from right and left will grow in strength.

4

False Economy

A four-hour drive westwards from Santo Domingo lies the coastal town of Barahona. With perhaps 50,000 inhabitants, it is a typical Dominican provincial centre. A few main streets are lined with shops, banks and government buildings, while spreading out from the town centre are neighbourhoods of ramshackle one-storey wooden houses and tiny corner grocery stores. Set in a dusty coastal plain, Barahona is clearly poor; services such as electricity and water are erratic, and the local schools and medical centres are dilapidated. But, at the same time, there is a strong sense of collective organisation. A regional church-funded radio station discusses social and political issues, bringing local people into the studio to air their grievances. A group of women have organised themselves into a powerful pressure group, campaigning for better services for working mothers. Peasants demanding land titles win active support from trade unions and church groups inside the town.

With its mixture of poverty and popular organisation, Barahona typifies the more depressed areas of the Dominican Republic. Inland from the town lie thousands of acres of sugar-cane, once the property of Trujillo and now owned by the state. The vast fields are bordered by occasional tracks or railway lines, and here are the squalid *bateyes* — isolated clusters of concrete dormitories, inhabited by Haitian immigrant cane-cutters. Just outside the older part of Barahona stands the local Industrial Free Zone (IFZ), a complex of labour-intensive assembly plants employing hundreds of women on very low wages. Down the coast towards Haiti, meanwhile, there are already signs of new tourist developments. A billboard welcomes visitors and investors to the country's latest El Dorado and a new road stretches down through remote villages to so-far unspoilt beaches. A modern international airport is planned.

Table: merchandise exports and US$ (millions) value 1989	
Ferronickel	372.0
Sugar	217.8
Gold and doré	88.8
Coffee	87.6
Cocoa	49.9

Source: Economist Intelligence Unit 1991-2

Barahona is almost a microcosm of the Dominican Republic. Relying on sugar, the IFZ and tourism, it reflects the country's dependence, past and present, on agriculture, cheap labour and the North American market.

Although sugar, IFZs and tourism are vital to the Dominican economy, there are other important sectors and activities. The country's natural resources are surprisingly varied and the economy highly diversified by Caribbean standards. Among its exports are gold and silver, nickel and bauxite, tobacco, cocoa and coffee. There is also an expanding agro-industrial sector, with export crops such as pineapples and winter vegetables destined for the US market.

Yet despite the range of economic activity in the Dominican Republic, unemployment and underemployment remain critically high and poverty widespread. Official estimates put unemployment at approximately 30 per cent of the workforce, with another 30 per cent underemployed. The so-called informal economy of casual labour, street vending and domestic service as well as remittances sent from abroad are essential for the survival of many Dominican families. This is in part the legacy of long-term underdevelopment, due to colonial misrule, dictatorship and foreign interference. Yet the current economic crisis cannot be simply explained in terms of historic misfortunes. It is also inseparable from the development model which has been pursued by Dominican governments since the end of the Trujillo dictatorship.

Bitter Cane

The Dominican Republic's sugar industry has been in steep decline for the last two decades. Once almost entirely owned by foreign interests, the industry was largely taken over by Trujillo from 1952 onwards, following the sharp rise in world sugar prices brought about by World War II and international shortages. Trujillo's twelve *ingenios* or mills were nationalised in 1961 after his assassination and from 1966 have

been run (and in four cases closed or sold off) by the state-owned State
Sugar Council (CEA).

The CEA, writes Roger Plant (1987:35) is 'a massive and notoriously
inefficient organisation, acting virtually as a state within a state'. It
exists alongside the private-sector sugar industry, made up of the
Central Romana (formerly owned by Gulf & Western) and the smaller
Dominican Vicini group as well as eight thousand *colonos* or smaller
cane-producing farmers who sell their crop to both the CEA and the
Central Romana. In the late 1980s the CEA controlled 113,000 hectares
of sugar-cane land and eight *ingenios*, employing approximately 60,000
people. The Central Romana owns approximately 57,000 hectares
(making it one of the largest sugar-producing units in the world), while
the Vicini group owns 12,000 hectares. The *colonos*, meanwhile account
for approximately 85,000 hectares. In all, twelve per cent of cultivated
land in the Dominican Republic is devoted to sugar production.

The state sugar sector has a lamentable reputation for
mismanagement and corruption. During the 1970s Balaguer placed
control of the CEA in the hands of various military officers who took
full advantage of opportunities for graft and embezzlement. The
system of awarding jobs to political allies has resulted in massive
over-staffing in the CEA management. In addition, successive
governments have sacrificed the CEA's interests to those of the private
sector, especially when the mighty Gulf & Western ran the Central
Romana. In 1979, for instance, the Guzmán administration handed
over a large Venezuelan sugar order from the CEA to Gulf & Western
even though the latter had sold its entire current supplies; Gulf &
Western merely bought CEA-produced sugar on the US market and
sold it to Venezuela at a 25 per cent mark-up. Affected by
incompetence, corruption and other factors such as sugar-cane disease,
the CEA is chronically indebted and unprofitable. In 1977 its
production costs were estimated at 10.3 cents per pound against a
world market price of 9.4 cents per pound. By the end of the 1980s, its
debts stood at approximately US$200 million.

Much worse than its inefficiency, however, has been the CEA's role
in the brutal treatment of Haitian *braceros* or cane-cutters. Since the
1920s Dominican sugar plantations have depended on the exploitation
of cheap labour from neighbouring Haiti. The systematic ill treatment
and abuse of Haitians in the sugar industry and elsewhere in the
Dominican Republic has been the subject of many reports from human
rights organisations. In the course of 1991, the issue gained
international attention when several detailed reports of labour and
human rights violations briefly threatened Dominican privileged
access to the US market (see chapter 5). The Balaguer regime's response
was to start a campaign of deportation of 'illegal' Haitians and to

increase the intimidation and harassment which Haitian immigrants experience on a daily basis.

The influx of cheap labour from Haiti has played a large part in keeping the moribund Dominican sugar industry alive. Until 1986 bilateral agreements between the Dominican and Haitian governments brought thousands of *braceros* across the border each year in order to work in the cutting season. These short-term contract workers joined the so-called *viejos* (old hands), some of whom live more or less permanently in the Dominican Republic's *bateyes* and in other areas. With the fall of the Duvalier dictatorship in 1986 and ensuing instability in Haiti the agreement was not renewed, leading to an acute shortage of labour in the sugar plantations. The Dominican response was to use the military to round up any Haitians inside the country — irrespective of age, legal status or existing employment — and to force them into working on the plantations. The conditions faced by Haitian workers and their role in the Dominican economy will be more fully described in the next chapter.

Those Dominicans who work in the sugar industry do not normally cut cane, regarding it as under-paid and excessively arduous work. The jobs held by Dominicans tend to be considerably less gruelling: supervising the *braceros*, weighing and transporting the cane, working in the mills and distribution points. But the CEA and the private-sector sugar companies are hardly more generous to their Dominican workers than to the Haitians. Wages are extremely low, and the CEA pleads poverty when its workers demand improvements in pay or conditions. The trade unions, after years of extreme repression, are presently tolerated but largely ignored by CEA management. With some exceptions, their activities are much more directed at Dominican *ingenio* workers than at the Haitian cane-cutters. Only the General Confederation of Workers (CGT) and its sugar workers' federation, FENAZUCAR, has made serious efforts to represent both Dominican and Haitian workers' interests.

Not even forced labour has made the Dominican sugar industry viable. This is in part due to government policy and corruption, but it also reflects the precarious nature of the international sugar market with its unpredictable quota systems and price structures. The main market for Dominican sugar has always been the US, but successive administrations in Washington have veered between free-market policies and attempts to protect US sugar producers by imposing tariffs and quotas on exporters such as the Dominican Republic. In addition, the development of sugar substitutes such as high fructose corn syrup means that traditional sugar production is threatened by cheaper and reportedly healthier alternatives.

Haitian cane-cutter, near Barahona. (Philip Wolmuth)

The world sugar market is dominated by special arrangements between producer and importing countries, failed attempts to stabilise free-market prices through international agreements and massive over-production. The result has been a series of peaks and troughs for the Dominican industry. The 'miracle years' were 1974-8; in 1975 Dominican sugar fetched 76 cents per pound in the US market. At this time, the country's bill for imported oil was only 60 per cent of sugar revenues, fuelling the boom in public works and foreign investment. By 1982, however, the price of sugar had plummeted to five cents per pound and the oil bill had risen to 133 per cent of sugar earnings.

As the slump intensified, the US introduced fees and tariffs on imported sugar to protect its own producers. Shocked by the long-term implications of this protectionism, the Guzmán regime asked the Reagan administration in 1981 to reintroduce the quota system which it had abandoned in 1974. Under this system a set amount of sugar was bought by the US at the same price given to domestic producers and this amount was divided among competing producer nations. When quotas were subsequently reintroduced in 1982 they were a disappointment to the Dominican Republic. Of the total 1983 import quota of 2.8 million tons, the Dominicans were allotted only 447,000 tonnes (or 492,590 US short tons) — less than half of their sales in the free-market boom of 1975.

Further disappointments were to follow. With demand falling and production rising in the US, the Dominican quota was reduced to 302,016 tons in 1986, 160,160 tons in 1987 and 123,200 tons in 1988. Later that year the trend was later slightly reversed because of drought in the US, and for the period January 1989-September 1990 the quota rose to 367,000 tons. For the year ending September 1991 the quota stood at 394,500 tons. This partial recovery of the Dominican Republic's quota was purely temporary, however, and in October 1991 Washington announced a reduction for 1991-2 of 34 per cent. The quota may well be reduced again or scrapped altogether by the US government which unilaterally determines all sugar imports.

In the face of such instability, the Dominican government has tried to find new markets for its sugar and to diversify agricultural production away from over-dependence on a single crop. When the 47 per cent cut in the US quota was announced in 1987, Balaguer responded with typical political pragmatism, signing a three-year agreement with the Soviet Union to export 50,000 tons per year. While receiving only eight cents per pound (below the quota price), Balaguer nonetheless had the satisfaction of causing consternation among State Department officials. Other current markets for Dominican sugar include Algeria and Morocco.

Diversification

Even though the world sugar market shows occasional signs of recovery, the long-term malaise of the Dominican industry has forced the government to seek alternatives. The crisis surrounding cheap Haitian labour has also dealt Dominican sugar a serious blow, with the 1991 CEA *zafra* (harvest period) producing a 35,000 ton shortfall on targets, following the record low total figure of 304,000 tons in 1990. The CEA announced in June 1991 that it intended to invest heavily in mechanised cane cutting equipment for the following *zafra*, but several newspapers pointed out that it had made many similar announcements frequently in the past. Meanwhile, total sugar exports in 1990 were valued at US$191 million, little more than a third of the 1981 figure of US$532 million.

The sugar crisis has prompted moves to produce other, non-traditional, agricultural exports for the US and European markets. Supported by grants from the US Agency for International Development (USAID), the CEA has entered into a joint venture with Frutas Dominicanas, a United Brands subsidiary, to produce pineapples for the US. The Dole Fruit Company, like United Brands a US agro-industrial multinational, has invested US$13.5 million in pineapple production, aiming to export 100,000 tons annually. Under the umbrella of the USAID-funded Joint Agribusiness Coinvestment Council, Dominican and foreign companies have invested an estimated US$300 million in the new agribusinesses which include melons, vegetables, citrus fruit and flowers. Some of the Dominican companies are new, run by a younger generation of technocrats and entrepreneurs. Others belong to the older land-owning families with interests in traditional exports such as sugar and rum.

Under the terms of the 1983 Caribbean Basin Initiative, non-traditional agricultural exports from the Dominican Republic enjoy duty-free access into the US market. This, together, with substantial tax concessions from the Dominican government, makes agribusiness an attractive proposition for US investors. The Dominican Republic's accession to the Lomé Convention in 1990 also gives the country duty-free entry into the EEC. Initial exports of bananas to the Ireland-based Fyffes company incurred the wrath of the Windward Islands' governments (Grenada, Dominica, St Lucia and St Vincent), since the Dominican Republic had formally undertaken not to use its Lomé membership to export bananas into the highly protected UK market. The Dominican government and Fyffes stress, however, that Dominican bananas, produced in the state-owned La Cruz de Manzanillo plantation, are exported to Belgium, Germany and Poland. According to the government, the first year of Lomé membership resulted in exports of coffee, tobacco and citrus fruits to the EEC worth US$20 million.

Yet the gradual switch away from sugar has not improved conditions for the poorest people in the Dominican countryside. Instead of using the unviable sugar land for agrarian reform (see box), the government has preferred to transfer ownership and resources to foreign agribusinesses and their Dominican partners. Dole, for instance, has taken over 5,000 hectares of former CEA land in Río Haina, Cotuí and Monte Plata, while Frutas Dominicanas has 4,000 hectares at the former Catarey *ingenio* at Villa Altagracia. In contrast, the state agency in charge of land reform has received a tiny fraction of such land. As a result, landlessness remains a pressing problem of landlessness is not addressed and domestic food production declined during the 1980s. Influential critics such as Bernardo Vega, former head of the Central Bank, also point out that CEA land around the larger cities and towns could more usefully be redeployed for low-cost housing.

The growing emphasis on new forms of large-scale export agriculture has also further marginalised the estimated 400,000 people dependent on coffee production. Traditionally, coffee is cultivated on smallholdings by family units with occasional employment given to

Agrarian Reform: Broken Promises

Since the death of Trujillo, all Dominican governments have stressed the importance of redistributing land and services to the poorest sectors of the Dominican peasantry. The Dominican Agrarian Institute (IAD), established in 1962 by the interim government with extensive US funding, held almost 375,000 hectares of land for this purpose. Although the initial plan to settle 25,000 families by 1967 and 70,000 by 1970 was hardly ambitious, it was never reached. The second figure was later reduced to 45,000 and by 1965 only 2,700 families had been settled on about 15,000 hectares.

Although the Bosch government included provision for land expropriation in its short-lived constitution, Balaguer subsequently refused to attack the large landowners' privileges. Despite the rhetoric of reform, the distribution of land proceeded slowly. In 1971, it was estimated that 216 Dominican families owned the same amount of land as 220,000 smallholders and that a further 200,000 families were landless (Stanfield 1989:311). While only 1,000 families had on average benefited annually from the reform, much bigger areas were turned over by the government to extensive cattle-raising on large *haciendas*.

The 1971 census, by revealing these statistics, forced Balaguer to take stronger measures. Legislation enabled the IAD to take over unoccupied land, abolished share-cropping and expropriated some large farms. The rate of redistribution accelerated for some years, and between 1972 and 1977 almost 330,000 hectares of land were handed out. But the laws concerning share-cropping and the large farms were never fully implemented, even though the IAD could have taken control of seven million hectares through legal expropriations. Since the 1970s, moreover, the pace of reform has again slowed down, failing to keep up with rural population growth. In the words of Adriano Sánchez Roa:

> When we see that over 27 years an annual average of 2,340 families have been settled, and that there are 514,000 more families asking for land, we have to face the sad truth that at this rate it would take more than two centuries just to hand out land titles.

migrant Haitian workers. These smallholdings are often situated in remote rural areas and receive little assistance in terms of infrastructure and credit from the state. A mere eight Dominican family firms dominate the export of coffee to the North American and European markets, while producers are regularly exploited by a structure of 'middlemen' who pay them as little as a fifth of the price they in turn receive from the export houses in Barahona, Azua, Peravia and several other towns. The state, too, takes a large cut in the form

Too Many People, Not Enough Land

'I come from a place called Puñal, not far from Santiago. Most people there are peasants, and although families are very big, the average smallholding is between 20 and 30 *tareas* (1-2 hectares). People grow food for everyday consumption — corn, beans, bananas — and some tobacco. It is a sort of subsistence economy, and most families have relatives in the US or in the city who send cash back so that the family can buy the things it cannot produce for itself.

Many families have at least five children and some as many as ten or fifteen. There is not enough land for all these people to work, so peasants try to send their sons to work on other people's land. A larger landowner who has, say, 50 or 80 *tareas* (3-5 hectares), may let some of his land in exchange for half the proceeds, or he may pay a daily wage of 20 to 30 *pesos*. That sum is not enough to buy food for one meal for a large family. Rice is now very expensive, and people are lucky if they eat meat once a week on Sunday. You can buy some basic things at the local store, but they are very expensive.

A big problem for the local peasants is transport. The roads are terrible and people cannot afford their own vehicles. Before, there were many horses, but now they are scarce, and peasants cannot carry one bag of bananas or cocoa to market in Santiago. As a result, middlemen with their lorries collect the fruit and vegetables and take them to the city. But they take about 50 per cent of the selling price.

There are too many people without enough land, and at the same time there is a great deal of unused land. Consequently, many Dominicans live in a state of permanent insecurity, not knowing how they will feed their families. Others leave the countryside for the city, or for New York, but most only discover a different sort of poverty there.'
Interview with David Vásquez, Priest in Dominican Order, Santo Domingo.

of high export taxes. The collapse of the International Coffee Agreement (a system of quotas designed to ensure a stable world price) in 1989 added to the coffee producers' difficulties, reducing export prices by 60 per cent (Sánchez Roa 1990:119).

With government support and finance going to the new agro-industries, the traditional export crops and their producers have fared badly. Like coffee, cocoa has historically been cultivated on small plots, with an estimated 84 per cent of producers farming holdings of less than five hectares. Cocoa farmers have little access to credit or services, and consequently yields per hectare and quality are extremely low. Three large exporting houses accounted for 79 per cent of overseas trade between 1979 and 1988. A similar monopoly of distribution exists in tobacco production, with small farmers forced to sell to a handful of exporters based primarily in Santiago. Dominican cigars are now considered a luxury item in the US and European markets, but high prices have not been passed on to small producers who have seen costs outstrip income during the 1980s.

A critical factor in the growing impoverishment of the small Dominican farmer has been the escalating costs of production in relation to the prices received for various crops. The government's policy of successive devaluation against the US dollar (see chapter 6) has resulted in spectacular increases in the prices of imported agricultural inputs such as machinery, fertiliser and pesticide. Between 1978 and 1988, for instance, the production costs for tobacco, coffee and cocoa rose by 407 per cent, 384 per cent and 286 per cent respectively. Meanwhile, the prices paid to the producers rose during the same decade by 389 per cent, 316 per cent and 158 per cent. With cocoa in particular, production costs have risen so sharply as to make its cultivation economically unviable.

The export-led restructuring of Dominican agriculture has so far served to reinforce the historic inequalities in land ownership and access to resources. The most recent agricultural census in 1981 revealed that two per cent of owners control 55 per cent of cultivable land, while 82 per cent of farmers own only 12 per cent (Sánchez Roa 1990:107). The gulf between the *minifundio* (smallholding) and *latifundio* (estate) actually grew wider between 1971 and 1981, with a greater concentration of land in fewer large properties and a further multiplication of small and economically unviable plots.

In contrast to the tiny and overworked plots of thousands of small farmers stand the sprawling cattle ranches which belong to a small number of wealthy landowners. Much of this land, accounting for almost 45 per cent of arable territory, is farmed extensively with relatively few animals per hectare. According to the National Office of Statistics, in 1981, 194 properties covering 340,000 hectares contained only two head of cattle per hectare. Of these properties, 38 were larger than 1,000 hectares in size. While the large *hacienda* is clearly a status symbol and proof of belonging to the landed gentry, it can also be a profitable concern. Beef exports to the US were worth more than US$36 million in 1988. At the same time, however, most Dominicans can rarely afford to eat meat.

The end result of the Dominican land tenure system is the continuing existence, as during the Trujillo dictatorship, of a land-hungry or landless 'rural proletariat'. The countryside offers the poor shrinking options: badly paid work in the non-traditional export sector, intermittent labour in other agriculture or dependence upon cheques sent by relatives abroad. Not surprisingly, more and more Dominicans

La Romana Industrial Free Zone. (Philip Wolmuth)

are leaving their villages and moving towards the cities in search of work and other opportunities. Others look to emigration, legal or illegal, as their only chance of economic survival.

Cheap Labour Inc
In today's Dominican Republic, almost every urban centre of any size has its own Industrial Free Zone (IFZ). Normally situated on the outskirts of town, the IFZ, an industrial park, is usually made up of a series of hangar-like buildings, surrounded by high fences and patrolled by security guards. The buildings are low-cost assembly plants, and each morning at 7.30am hundreds, and often thousands, of local workers, overwhelmingly women, stream into the plants to start a 10-hour day of repetitive and poorly-paid labour.

The companies situated in the IFZs are involved principally in textiles, footwear, sports goods, electronics, pharmaceuticals and the increasingly important areas of data processing and other service industries. Approximately 90 per cent of capital investment in the IFZs is foreign, mainly from the US. Large companies such as Westinghouse operate in the San Cristóbal industrial park, sending electrical goods back to the US via Puerto Rico. A subsidiary of American Airlines,

Pandora's Box

'Somebody suggested that I went to another factory...to Pandora Fashion. At Pandora Fashion I was well thought of, my work was appreciated.

There they made shirts, different sorts of shirts and those headbands that people wear when they're playing sports. These bands are made of towelling material and when they're sown they produce a sort of dust which asphyxiates the women and makes them cough. The owner did nothing about it, there was no ventilation, and with the heat and the dust people were suffocating. It was really unbearable. Sometimes you saw a woman who had fainted being carried out. The working conditions and hygiene were terrible.

In that factory I worked as a supervisor, passing the good work and sending back the bad work. As well as the bad conditions, I had a lot of problems concerning overtime. I would say that "extras" are the biggest problem in San Pedro de Macorís and free trade zones generally, because people simply don't understand that sometimes you can't work any more. They don't care if you've got sick children, and even after a full day's work it's expected of you to stay on if they want you to.'
Interview with Teodora Espinosa, IFZ worker, San Pedro de Macorís.
(Pineda 1990:27-8)

Caribbean Data Services, is engaged in processing data such as airline ticket reservations in San Isidro IFZ near Santo Domingo. Other investors have come from Taiwan, Hong Kong and South Korea and are mostly involved in textile exports to the US market.

Few Dominican raw materials are involved in this form of manufacturing and links with the rest of the national economy are minimal, although the government has proposed greater coordination between IFZs and the domestic market. Instead, the raison d'etre of the IFZs is cheap labour. In 1991 IFZ-based companies employed some 130,000 Dominicans, approximately eight per cent of the national workforce, in a range of labour-intensive and repetitive activities such as sewing parts of clothing together or assembling electrical components. Through inflation and devaluation, the country has become the one of cheapest labour sources in the entire region, as cheap even as Haiti. The hourly rate fell in real terms from US$1 in 1986 to 35 US cents in 1990. In late 1990, an average IFZ worker took home 700 or 800 *pesos* per month, including some hours of overtime. At the prevailing official exchange rate of 11.20 *pesos* to the dollar, this was equivalent to a monthly salary of between US$62.50 and US$71.50. A daily wage in the Dominican Republic is therefore less than a very poor hourly rate in the US.

In order to earn this wage, a Dominican IFZ worker typically works from 7.30am to 5 or 6pm with a 10-minute morning break and a half-hour lunch break. The work is intense and tedious; workers must meet hourly production targets, and the heat and noise are oppressive. Most workers are women, 18-25 years old and newly arrived from the countryside, whose only other work possibility is as a domestic servant. There are no child-care facilities, subsidised canteens are rare and transport costs from the towns to the IFZs must be met by the workers themselves. There are no prospects for promotion; instead, women are commonly sacked after three or four years in order to make way for younger workers. Initially, the workers undergo a period of up to six months of apprenticeship — clearly unnecessary for the rudimentary work they do — but are paid half the minimum wage during this time (Consultoras Asociadas 1989:39).

Trade unions are effectively banned inside the IFZs. In its 1990 workers' rights review, the US Trade Policy Staff Committee looking into the Dominican Republic's eligibility for US Generalized System of Preferences benefits heard evidence from the US union confederation, AFL-CIO:

> Despite government assurances that workers in the free trade zones would have the right to organize and bargain collectively, workers in those zones who recently attempted to organize unions were summarily fired. Workers were fired from Westinghouse, Sylvania, Hanes and several other local companies after they began to organize unions. In Westinghouse, the union was able to gain legal recognition; however three weeks later all nine of the union leaders were fired. With a weak labour code and judicial system, there is little expectation that any of those workers will be reinstated.

In May 1991 Paul Somogyi, a Latin America specialist for the AFL-CIO, compared the IFZs to 'mini-dictatorships'. Claiming that the AFL-CIO had unsuccessfully tried to encourage unions in the IFZs, he complained that 'people are fired overnight and are not even allowed to mention trade unions in those zones.'

The IFZs first came to the Dominican Republic in 1969 through Gulf & Western which was trying to diversify its interests in the country by locating subsidiaries around its huge Central Romana complex. A few others followed, notably in San Pedro de Macorís, but these early plants were government-controlled and were geared more towards the prevailing industrial policy of import substitution for the domestic market than towards exports.

The boom really began in 1985 after two economic developments which confirmed a growing trend towards export-led policies. The first was the application in 1984 of the Caribbean Basin Initiative, with its structure of duty-free access into the US market for manufactured goods from the region. The second, following the controversial intervention of the International Monetary Fund (see chapter 6), was the devaluation of the Dominican *peso* in 1985. This ended the official dollar-*peso* parity which had artificially overvalued the Dominican currency and immediately reduced costs for foreign companies operating in the Dominican Republic by as much as 30 per cent as well as making exports more competitive. The change in Dominican exchange rate policy also coincided with a series of legislative initiatives which further opened up the country to foreign investment. These involved tax concessions, the right for foreign companies to repatriate profits and assured infrastructural investment by the government. The Dominican private sector also became involved at this stage, and now administers the majority of IFZs.

Attracted by the liberalisation of the Dominican economy, foreign investors rushed to take advantage of the range of new incentives. The number of IFZs increased at once from four in 1983 to 22 in 1991. By the end of 1990 there were more than 300 companies operating within the country. In that year, the value of IFZ exports to the US rose to US$771.32 million, according to the Dominican Centre for Export Promotion. The government has stated that it hopes the sector will employ 350,000 people by 1994.

The proponents of IFZs claim that they bring jobs and foreign exchange to the Dominican Republic. They point out, for instance, that the siting of the IFZs around the country generates regional employment and deters migration to Santo Domingo. The government also stresses the contribution to foreign-exchange earnings made by the IFZ companies which pay dollars into the Central Bank and receive *pesos* in order to pay wages and other overheads. In 1989, for example, these revenues came to US$190 million.

But critics of the IFZs have shown that low-wage assembly work brings few long-term benefits to the economy. Low wages do not enable workers to consume more locally produced goods and hence create few 'forward linkages' with other sectors of the economy. There is little transfer of technology from the company to the host country, since manufacturing is usually labour-intensive and complex jobs are filled by foreign staff. Additionally, export-processing industries such as textiles generate less foreign exchange than do traditional commodities because so much of the material involved is imported. Machinery is imported duty-free, and the textiles themselves are actually manufactured elsewhere and merely assembled in the IFZs. Unrestricted profit repatriation means that foreign companies do not invest in the country, while tax concessions prevent the Dominican government from collecting badly needed revenue. The end result is the creation of 'footloose' offshore companies, with few long-term commitments to the Dominican Republic, which can move easily to new host countries in the event of political instability or rising labour costs.

It is debatable whether the IFZs can viably replace even the ailing sugar industry as the Dominican Republic's economic lifeline. As Carmen Diana Deere *et al* (1990:181) conclude, the low value-added component of export-processing industries makes them highly inefficient generators of foreign exchange and employment in comparison to traditional agricultural exports:

> According to a recent GAO [US General Accounting Office] report, traditional exports such as sugar and coffee have an estimated value-added component of 90 per cent, while light manufacturing, such as garments, has a value-added component of approximately 20 per cent. Thus, a $1 million decline in sugar exports would have to be offset by a $4.5 million increase in garment exports to maintain the same level of value-added and to generate the same net foreign exchange. According to their calculations, to maintain similar employment levels, a $1 million reduction in sugar exports would have to be compensated by a $6 million increase in textile exports.

Furthermore, the planned North American Free Trade Agreement between the US, Canada and Mexico threatens to remove the Dominican Republic's comparative advantage in labour costs and duty-free access. With cheap labour and duty-free access from Mexico guaranteed, US companies could no longer see the Dominican Republic as such a good deal.

Poor Man's Paradise

The Dominican Republic's beach resorts are a world away from the sugar plantations and factories, even though in a town such as La Romana the cane fields stretch up to the perimeter fence of the luxury hotel complex. Here, in the exclusive Casa de Campo, the tourists pay up to US$600 per day to play golf or polo and to enjoy a beach which is closed to locals. It is the up-market end of Dominican tourism, attracting wealthy North Americans who can land their private planes on the resort's airstrip. Further round the south-east coast is the mass-market destination of Punta Cana. At the nearby 1,000-room Bávaro Beach resort charter flights from the UK bring hundreds of British tourists at low-budget all-inclusive prices. Within ten years the

Chasing the tourist dollar in Santo Domingo. (Philip Wolmuth)

remote south-west tip of the country has been transformed into a booming tourist area, with its own international airport.

The Dominican Republic is a latecomer to the Caribbean tourist industry. Few visitors were tempted by its reputation during the Trujillo period and the US invasion of 1965 did little to improve its image. However, the creation in 1966 of a National Tourist Board and the introduction in 1971 and 1972 of state incentives and credit to the industry attracted some investment from the government and private sector. As with the IFZs, it was the devaluation of the *peso* in 1985 and the resulting lowering of costs which brought in foreign and domestic capital. Between 1985 and 1989, 12,000 hotel rooms came into operation and the number of visitors almost doubled from 753,000 to 1,400,000. By the end of 1992, according to the government, the country will receive more than 1,500,000 tourists with an infrastructure of 23,000 hotel rooms and five international standard airports. At this rate, the Dominican Republic is poised to overtake the Bahamas as the biggest tourist destination in the Caribbean.

Tourists come to the Dominican Republic for the same reasons as to any other Caribbean destination: sunshine, beaches and a taste of the exotic. But they also choose the country in increasing numbers because it is significantly cheaper than other comparable Caribbean tourist centres. A two-week holiday in the Dominican Republic can cost as little as £400 or £500, thus rivalling many European destinations for price. The Dominican Republic is cheaper because wages are lower, and labour is an important part of this service industry's overheads. Few workers in the Dominican tourist business earn the national minimum monthly wage of 1,000 *pesos* and most earn much less. The cooks, waiters, cleaners, receptionists and other workers, mostly women, make up a low-wage labour force with little job security or prospects of promotion. Trade unions are unheard-of, and high rates of unemployment are a deterrent to workers' demands for higher wages.

As with the IFZs, foreign capital underpins Dominican tourism. Names such as Sheraton and Club Med are conspicuous in the country, and the vast former Gulf & Western complex at La Romana is controlled by the Florida-based Fanjul family consortium. Successive Dominican governments have offered generous incentives to foreign investors (another reason for the country's relative cheapness). Current attractions include 10-year exemptions on income, corporate and local tax as well as duty-free imports of goods not locally available. According to the *El Caribe* newspaper, the government has made some astonishing concessions to foreign firms. A 30-year lease on the up-market Jaragua hotel in Santo Domingo was allegedly sold to the US Transamerican Hotel company at the rate of 60,000 *pesos* per month. After 30 years, it has been estimated, the government will receive 21.6 million *pesos*, while the company will make on a single suite (of which there are 350) a sum of 89 million *pesos* (Rudel 1989:112).

The private-sector tourist investment agency, Proinversión, claims that tourism has created 20,000 direct jobs nationally and a further 70,000 indirect jobs, in sectors such as transport, catering and furnishing. According to its president, Rafael Blanco Canto, hotels and restaurants use local food and 70 cents of every US dollar spent in the Dominican Republic remains in the country. He also stresses that tourism brings jobs to otherwise economically depressed areas such as Barahona and Punta Cana.

Others are less enthusiastic about tourism's contribution to the country's development. Government spending on infrastructure, for instance, has been aimed at tourist areas and facilities (airports, resorts, 'beautification' projects), neglecting basic services such as water supply and access roads in poor rural and urban areas. As a result, tourist zones operate as enclaves within wider areas of deprivation, often providing their own private electricity and water supply and literally fenced off from the surrounding community. While tourism does provide a degree of 'trickle-down' income for certain Dominicans such as taxi-drivers and restaurateurs, it is much more debatable whether it brings financial benefits to a wider social spectrum. With profit repatriation and tax-breaks on offer to foreign investors, much of the money generated by the large transnational operators leaves the country. In many cases, moreover, where holidays are prepaid in the tourists' own country, little of the money ever reaches the Dominican Republic.

Nevertheless, according to the Central Bank, tourism generated US$900 million of foreign income in 1990, amounting to 40 per cent of total exports of goods and services. If the government's hopes that the Columbus quincentenary attracts more tourists are realised, this sum is likely to increase still further.

Yet, with increased tourism come further social costs. The growing incidence of prostitution in the Dominican Republic, and the dramatic increase in AIDS cases, is one symptom of tourism's malign influence. A culture of envy and resentment is another result, as many young Dominicans seek to make a living, legal or not, on the fringes of the tourist industry. Shoe-shiners, self-appointed guides and illegal money-changers are all in pursuit of the elusive tourist dollar. The costs are also environmental. Rare mangrove swamps and forests have been destroyed to make way for new resorts. According to the Dominican Federation of Ecological Associations, approximately one million trees are to be cut down in the construction of a single golf course at Punta Cana. Already lagoons have been poisoned in order to eradicate mosquitoes, and sewage from beach-side hotels is pumped directly into the sea.

From Bad to Worse?

In the short term, at least, the Dominican economy seems set to revolve around the erratic sugar industry, the growth of new agribusinesses, IFZs and tourism. In addition, there is the foreign-exchange gained from mining, most notably ferro-nickel and gold. In 1989, high nickel prices brought in US$372 million, but in 1990 average price per pound dropped from US$5.83 to US$3.89, cutting earnings to US$262 million. By the end of 1991 Falconbridge Dominicana had halved production due to low world prices.

Gold, meanwhile, is declining rapidly, as the Pueblo Viejo mine, nationalised by the PRD government in 1979, nears exhaustion. 1989 yields were 50 per cent lower than the previous year's, and the government is trying to attract foreign companies to exploit what it claims are further ore finds worth US$5 billion.

Each of these activities, in its own way, offers a highly precarious economic future. Sugar may well become obsolete in the face of alternative sweeteners and changing dietary habits, while the interests

All in the Family

Foreign capital and interests play an important part in the the Dominican Republic. But alongside the US multinationals, the real power-brokers are the members of the Dominican elite. In 1966, Juan Bosch estimated that 5,000 families effectively ran the country, controlling state-run industries, financial institutions and private-sector business.

In the 1990s, the established elite have largely ridden the dramatic changes in the Dominican Republic's economic structure. The old oligarchy, based largely in Santiago, has diversified its interests, joining new entrepreneurs and foreign investors in the boom industries of export manufacturing and tourism. Several household names, from the heyday of the sugar barons, are still at the forefont of Dominican business:

The Bermúdez family, famous for their rum, are involved in banking, IFZs, motor imports and tourism.

The Vicini-Cabral family, the country's richest, still export sugar, but have diversified into textiles, construction materials, cattle and hotels.

The Barceló family, rum-producing rivals to the Bermúdez dynasty, are involved in agro-industry, banking and construction. They have invested heavily in the Bávaro Beach complex.

Economic and political power go hand in hand. Vice-President Carlos Morales Troncoso is a major share-holder in the Central Romana consortium and his family has interests in cattle and tourism. Formerly Gulf & Western's Dominican general manager, he was also head of the CEA between 1986 and 1989. The wealthy 'Santiago oligarchy' has provided many political leaders and a number of presidents — Guzmán and Jorge Blanco, for instance. This closely interrelated and exclusive clique wields influence not only in the old export and new service industries, but equally in state agencies such as CORDE, INESPRE, and the CEA. It also controls much of the Dominican media — newpapers, television channels and advertising companies.

Source: Rosario (1988)

of Third World producers inevitably come second to those of the First World. The new export crops, from avocados to pineapples, also depend upon foreign tastes and fashions and must compete with identical exports from other producers in Latin America and Africa. Mining, too, is subject to volatile world demand and prices, and like all extractive industries is non-sustainable.

What the agricultural sector, old and new, has in common with the growing services sector, is its reliance on cheap labour. While sugar and other Dominican crops have for decades relied upon plentiful supplies of Haitian migrants, the very existence of IFZs and, to a lesser extent, tourism, is based on the low wages paid to those Dominicans who work in such jobs. Should wages and other operating costs rise, the companies which have set up in the IFZs will simply move on to another, more cost-effective locale. To this extent, export-led manufacturing seems to provide few prospects of long-term development for the poor. Tourism, while based on a greater degree of capital investment, is also notoriously unreliable as a stable development strategy. The case of Haiti, where the AIDS epidemic and political instability destroyed the tourist trade, is a case in point.

Economic policy since Trujillo's death has barely improved the lot of the vast majority of Dominicans. While the country has moved from an overwhelmingly agricultural economy to one based on manufacturing and services, these changes have not brought prosperity to anyone other than a small elite of entrepreneurs and technocrats.

In thirty years, the near-slavery of the sugar plantation has largely given way to the low-wage economy of the export-processing zone. None of the major Dominican political parties has opposed this process. During the 1990 election campaign, the three principal parties all endorsed the move towards the new industries, while Balaguer and the PRD argued as to who should claim more credit for the boom in the IFZs.

Faced with these grim economic prospects, increasing numbers of Dominicans are seeking a better life abroad, either legally or illegally. At the same time, Haitians, for fifty years the mainstay of the Dominican Republic's sugar industry, are again being treated as scapegoats, responsible for unemployment and low wages. The next chapter looks in greater detail at these two interrelated aspects of the Dominican crisis.

5

Heaven and Hell

The northern tip of Manhattan houses the second biggest Dominican community after Santo Domingo. Spreading down from the northernmost district of Washington Heights, some 50 blocks of New York city are almost exclusively Dominican. Spanish is the lingua franca, and shops and restaurants, referring to regions of the Dominican Republic, bear names such as *'mi pequeño Cibao'*. The district's commercial activities reflect the tastes and concerns of its inhabitants. Shops selling *merengue* tapes stand next to travel agencies offering cheap three-hour flights to Santo Domingo and guaranteed delivery of money orders to any Dominican address within 48 hours. Such is the cultural impact of the Dominican population in upper Manhattan that the area has been unofficially renamed 'Quisqueya Heights'.

Meanwhile, in Santo Domingo, another exile community has left its unmistakeable stamp on the city. Around the so-called Model Market and the bustling shopping street of the Avenida Duarte is the area known as 'little Haiti'. Here, Haitian traders load up the brightly painted vehicles which will make the perilous 300 kilometre journey to the neighbouring capital, Port-au-Prince, carrying food and plastic household implements. The same lorries have brought in cheap clothing and shoes which Haitian vendors, mostly women, sell at knock-down prices. Elsewhere in the city, groups of Haitians try to sell paintings or statuettes to passing tourists.

In the Dominican Republic, migration is a two-way process. Up to a million Dominicans live in the US and Puerto Rico, while anything from 500,000 to a million Haitians are to be found in the Dominican Republic. The double diaspora is directly related to another paradox. Although rural unemployment in the Dominican Republic can reach 40 per cent, there are never enough workers to cut cane in the plantations. As a result, imported — and often forced — labour has been brought into the country to do work that Dominicans reject as beneath contempt. The reasons for the Dominican exodus to the US and the Haitian presence in the Dominican Republic are therefore broadly the same: poverty and the quest for a better life. Furthermore, if Dominicans encounter prejudice and lack of opportunities in the US, then Haitians are confronted with much worse in the Dominican Republic.

Dominicans in the US

Of the estimated one million Dominicans living in the US, almost 400,000 live in New York, where they make up the second largest Hispanic group after Puerto Ricans. Most of these are legal migrants with the right to live and work indefinitely in the US. But increasing numbers are *indocumentados*, having obtained student or tourist visas and deliberately overstayed their allotted period. Other illegal migrants come via Puerto Rico with bogus documents, claiming to be Puerto Rican and therefore automatically entitled to residency in the US. The growth in the numbers of *indocumentados* is a result of tougher restrictions by the US authorities. In 1990, for instance, the US consulate in Santo Domingo turned down 80 per cent of the 140,000 applications for visas of all sorts.

Dominican emigration has steadily increased in the course of the 1980s, reflecting the mounting economic crisis in the country. During the Trujillo period, emigration was strictly discouraged, but successive Dominican governments have done little to stop the flow of would-be exiles. Instead, evidence suggests that the Dominican authorities, notably the navy, actively connive with the organisers of illegal emigration in return for commission.

The Dominican community in New York has been described as an 'ethnic enclave', with its own self-contained economic system. Many better-established Dominicans operate small businesses such as shops, restaurants and travel agencies, while newer arrivals do piece work sewing at home or work in some part of the informal sector such as taxi-driving. Exploitation and poor wages are rife. The Dominican community is also forced into what is often sub-standard housing, where landlords take advantage of their tenants' ignorance about their legal rights. When Dominicans are *indocumentados*, they are unable to seek official assistance in disputes and have to tolerate overcrowding and high rents. The following *merengue* reflects a jaundiced view of life in New York:

Aquí la vida no vale   Here life is not worth
una guayaba podrida   a rotten guava
Si un tigre no te mata   If a hoodlum doesn't kill you
te mata la factoría   the factory will

(Georges 1990:225)

A handful of Dominicans, however, achieve their economic ambitions and are able to make enough money to live luxuriously in the US and to send back remittances to relatives in the Dominican Republic. One route to wealth for poor Dominicans has traditionally been that of sport. Since the US invasion of 1916, baseball has been the Dominican national sport and the country has supplied many top-level players to the US professional leagues. A top-ranking baseball player can command contracts worth millions of dollars and will often reinvest some of this money in his home town.

Another lucrative economic activity is the drug trade. According to Dominican community leaders in New York, Washington Heights has become a centre for the selling of the cocaine derivative, crack, and many young Dominicans are attracted by the money to be made in this business. Here, however, Dominicans must compete with other drug-dealing interests and tend to operate at the bottom of the hierarchy, selling crack on the streets. The human toll is high; in 1990 more than 100 young Dominicans died violently on the streets of New York. Although lethal, the drug-trade can be very profitable, especially for those higher in the distribution structure. Several Dominican towns — notably San Francisco de Macorís and Baní — are reputed to owe many of their new housing complexes and BMWs to the crack industry. Much more money is reported also to come into the country through its role as a drug trans-shipment point between South America and the US and as a money-laundering centre.

The great majority of Dominicans, however, must work long hours in factories or service industries to earn enough money to send back to their families. Because of the informal nature of the remittance economy, it is impossible to assess accurately how much money enters the Dominican Republic in this way, but estimates range from US$500 million (Kryzanek and Wiarda 1988:112) to more than US$900 million. In either case, this sum amounts to more than the combined Dominican earnings from sugar and ferronickel.

The Remittance Economy

Regular monthly sums of US$50 or US$100 keep many rural families in the Dominican Republic above the poverty line. In many cases, a family sends a member abroad to join relations or community contacts in order to earn this regular income. Parents often have to leave young children behind, and send money home to cover their needs and, if necessary, to reimburse the non-relative who looks after them. Sometimes, larger amounts are needed, in order to pay for a medical operation or a new piece of farm machinery. More often than not,

Waiting for Dollars

'Although geographically close to Santiago, the three *sierra* towns of Jánico, San José de las Matas and Monción are almost entirely dependent — economically — on the far-off and foreign city of New York. Every day is like a quiet Sunday in these small communities, and the peaceful routine is only broken on special dates such as Christmas. This inactivity can only be explained by the fact that people are content to wait for the dollars from New York which will cover all their needs.

Almost every family has a member in the big city, and some are all there together, leaving their house locked up behind them. This phenomenon affects every social and economic feature of these communities and is responsible for the clear disincentive to study or work. The small-scale enterprises which employ local people and bring money into the region are the work of poor self-motivated entrepreneurs who have never lived outside the country. Nowhere is there evidence that a business or factory is the result of investment from those who have gone abroad. Perhaps the only sign is a car wash being set up in Monción.

Small towns with big-city tastes. This is the legacy of those who head north. A subtle, but tangible influence in fashion, with "Lakers" or "Hawks" basketball gear... Here, according to a youth from Jánico, is where fashion and the new videos arrive first, even before they are shown in the capital city's cinemas.'

Ultima Hora 17 July 1990

however, remittances merely cover everyday consumption, and the small surplus is lent to other families or invested in house repairs or livestock. As a result, the remittance economy is largely non-productive in development terms, generating little economic activity or employment other than trade in the home community.

If migrants' remittances contribute little to the long-term development of rural areas, nor for the most part does their return. Most returning migrants, particularly legal ones, prefer to invest their money in urban business ventures, in Santo Domingo or Santiago. Many, according to Eugenia Georges (1990:220), rarely return to their original communities. It is primarily the undocumented, and unsuccessful, migrants who return home.

The Mona Passage

While most Dominican emigrants see New York as their promised land, there are other favoured destinations. In 1991 the Dominican press printed several lurid stories about the trade in prostitutes from the Dominican Republic to Greece and other European and Caribbean countries. An indignant editorial in the *Hoy* newspaper accused the Dominican authorities of complicity in allowing women to go to Venezuela, Colombia, Spain, Italy, Holland and Greece to work as 'dancers'. According to a women's organisation in Barahona, literally hundreds of women from the depressed communities of the south-west have gone to Europe as prostitutes in order to send back money to their families.

Perhaps the most desperate form of emigration involves a 70-mile boat trip from the eastern tip of the Dominican Republic across the Mona Passage to Puerto Rico. For between US$250 and US$500 a Dominican illegal immigrant can book a place in a *yola*, a tiny fishing boat which makes the crossing. Sometimes the boat never arrives, leaving the disappointed passengers no means of recovering their investment. More frequently the boat is intercepted en route to Puerto Rico and the Dominicans returned to their own country. In 1990, US coastguard patrols intercepted 3,800 Dominicans in Puerto Rican waters. Occasionally the attempt to escape ends in tragedy. The flimsy *yolas*, overloaded with passengers, can easily capsize and the Mona Passage is notorious for its sharks. In 1987 a single shipwreck resulted in the loss of 70 lives.

The emigration business is lucrative for the ironically nicknamed 'consuls' who own the boats and arrange the trips as well as their scouts (*buscones*) who recruit likely passengers in cities and villages around the country. The Dominican navy which theoretically patrols the Mona Passage is also frequently accused of taking bribes for turning a blind eye to the trade.

Once in Puerto Rico, Dominicans look for work or try to acquire a false birth certificate and then go on to the US itself. The process of bribing an official may cost as much as a further US$3,000. Many *indocumentados* are picked up at this stage and returned to the Dominican Republic; authorities in San Juan reported the deportation of 14,900 Dominicans in 1990. According to the Dominican authorities, over 110,000 migrants have crossed the Mona Passage since 1980. Of these 30 per cent have succeeded in remaining in Puerto Rico or reached the US, 60 per cent were intercepted and ten per cent died in the attempt. An estimated 80,000 Dominicans are permanently settled in Puerto Rico, many employed as domestic workers or involved in informal-sector trading.

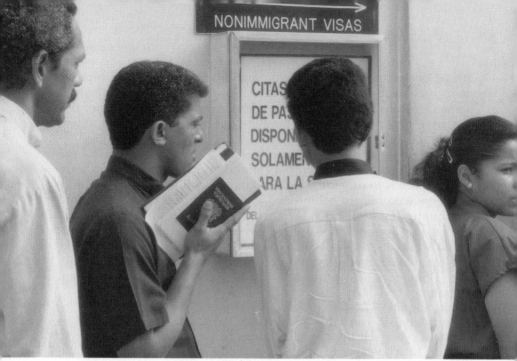

Queuing for visas at the US Embassy, Santo Domingo.   (Julio Etchart)

Researchers disagree as to whether the majority of Dominican migrants are from rural or urban backgrounds. It has been suggested, for instance, that those from the poorest rural sectors do not have the financial means to undertake the trip. Other research, however, indicates that family members already in the US or Puerto Rico send money for this purpose. The Puerto Rican sociologist, Jorge Duany, makes a clear distinction between those Dominicans who reach New York and those who remain in Puerto Rico. The former are, on average, better educated, from urban backgrounds and were employed before leaving; the latter are more likely to be from poorer rural communities with high levels of unemployment. Many more women than men, moreover, migrate. According to Duany, three out of every five Dominican migrants are women (*El Siglo* 1 October 1990). With the deteriorating economic situation in the Dominican Republic, it is also evident that significant numbers of middle-class professionals,such as health workers and teachers, are tempted by the prospect of escape.

Migration and Development

A much-repeated Dominican TV advertisement for rum portrays a young man working in a factory in New York but dreaming of the girl he has left behind in his Dominican village. Suddenly, on impulse, he throws away his overalls, walks out of the factory and in the next scene is reunited with the girl in an idyllic rural scene. Images of this sort may appeal to separated families, but bear little relation to real experiences of migration and exile.

Migration is above all a survival strategy, a response to the deepening economic crisis in the Dominican Republic. Its short-term consequence is to provide a higher standard of living for those family members who remain behind and an influx of foreign exchange into the country (most of which is transferred into *pesos* through the black market and does little to ease the government's shortage of dollars). It also acts as a safety valve in a country of high unemployment levels. The remittances and alleviation of unemployment may well explain the Dominican government's ambivalence concerning illegal migration.

But migration is not only a symptom of poverty and lack of opportunity; it can also exacerbate these conditions. Would-be migrants often sell their smallholdings to larger farmers in order to finance their escape to the US, thereby adding to the unequal distribution of land in the countryside. The remittance economy acts as a disincentive to agricultural work which, coupled with the absence of younger people from farming communities, reduces local food production. The disappearance of educated and qualified Dominicans, furthermore, amounts to a 'brain drain'. According to one researcher, the 5,125 Dominicans admitted to the US between 1969 and 1974 with managerial and professional qualifications made up 45 per cent of the country's higher education output for that period (Georges 1990:239).

Migration overseas is only a part of a wider process of economically motivated movement. For many Dominican *campesinos*, the first stage towards a better life is reaching a large town — Santo Domingo, Santiago, Puerto Plata — where opportunities and services are likely to be better. Only later does migration to the US or Puerto Rico become a viable option. Consequently, the phenomena of rural poverty and migration abroad are often joined by a middle stage of urban experience which may prepare the would-be migrant for the trip overseas. Many, of course, go no further than the city and join the swelling *cordones de miseria* ('poverty belts') or shantytowns around Santo Domingo.

The Haitian Exodus

Poverty is relative. The Dominican Republic is poor, but Haiti is poorer still. In 1989 the World Bank estimated the Dominican Republic's per capita GDP at US$957 and Haiti's at US$319. For every 145 Dominicans per square kilometre there are estimated to be 226 Haitians. In every statistical sense, Haiti is more unequal, more unhealthy and more underdeveloped than its neighbour. Nowhere is this disparity more strikingly visible than flying over the border. On the Dominican side there are still forests on the mountains, decreasing in area annually, but still clearly in evidence. On the Haitian side, there is nothing but scarred and eroded hillsides. Land shortages and poverty have pushed Haitian peasants high into the hills to cut wood for charcoal. Now, nothing will grow on the eroded land.

Haitians have been coming to work in the Dominican Republic since the US occupation of both countries (Haiti was invaded in 1915 and the marines remained until 1934). Their first destinations were the US-controlled sugar plantations which massively expanded during the period, requiring an influx of cheap labour. Hitherto at the beginning of the century, the Dominican sugar industry had imported labourers from the English-speaking territories of Jamaica, the Virgin Islands, the Turks and Caicos and the eastern Caribbean islands of St Kitts-Nevis and Anguilla. These workers were known as *cocolos* and some of their descendants, bearing English names, are still to be found in areas such as San Pedro de Macorís.

Dominicans have always refused to cut cane. Historians argue that this is a historically determined response to work associated with the humiliations of slavery. Yet the Dominican Republic was the one Caribbean sugar-producer never to have a slave-based plantation system, and what few slaves there were were mostly engaged in cattle-raising or other forms of agriculture. Instead, sugar only became central to the Dominican economy at the beginning of the 20th century, when slavery had long since been abolished. But since the introduction of the sugar economy, pay and conditions on the plantations have always been abysmal, and this basic economic reality probably explains the Dominican aversion to cane-cutting more than anything else.

Haitian migration to work in the Dominican sugar industry began in earnest in the 1930s, when the official census of 1935 recorded more than 50,000 Haitians in the Dominican Republic. At this time, Trujillo had not yet developed personal interests in sugar and hence saw the presence of thousands of Haitians more as a political and racial problem than an economic advantage. In the wake of the Great Depression, when sugar prices plummeted, Cuba expelled thousands of its Haitian cane-cutters, and many fled to the Dominican Republic. While the US sugar companies survived the virtual collapse of the world market by depending on the Haitians, Trujillo was more interested in issuing a political warning to Haiti, from which the US authorities had withdrawn in 1934. Complaining that Haitian workers were responsible for unemployment and low wages in towns such as Barahona and Pedernales, Trujillo spoke of the need for the 'Dominicanisation' of the border. In 1945, Balaguer, by now an ideologue for the Trujillo regime, looked back at the Dominican government's attitude towards the 'Haitian problem':

> ...by 1935 there were 400,000 Haitians in our country, resulting in the corrosion of national solidarity; voodoo, a kind of African animism of the lowest origins, became the preferred cult among Dominicans of the border area. The *gourde* [Haitian currency] replaced the *peso*. Peasants were learning from the Haitians anti-Christian customs, such as incestuous unions. We were about to be absorbed by Haiti. (Fiehrer 1990:11)

In October 1937, Trujillo ordered the Dominican armed forces to begin the massacre of all Haitians they could find inside the Dominican Republic. No precise tally of the victims exists, but between 10,000 and 20,000 Haitians — men, women and children — were murdered. Only those who were actually inside the US-owned sugar enclaves were spared, Trujillo fearing to upset the powerful companies which needed Haitian labour. Many others escaped back into Haiti during several days of terror and confusion.

When news of the massacre reached the outside world, there was more indifference than outrage. An international commission of enquiry eventually reported on the killings, and Trujillo agreed to pay compensation to the Haitian government of US$750,000. In the event, Trujillo paid only US$525,000 which was pocketed by the authorities in Port-au-Prince.

Official Slavery

The 1937 massacre did little to stop the migration of Haitians to the Dominican sugar industry. As Trujillo took personal control of much of the industry, he acquired a steady supply of Haitian labour by means of a bilateral contract with the Haitian government. Under the first *convenio* of 1952, 16,500 Haitians were brought over. Subsequent agreements were made between Trujillo and 'Papa Doc' Duvalier and later between the CEA and 'Baby Doc' Duvalier. From 1979 onwards the CEA dealt directly with the Haitian government; the terms of the contracts were never discussed by the Dominican legislature. In each case, the Haitian government was handsomely paid for 'expenses' incurred in the recruitment and transportation of *braceros* to the Dominican border. During the 1980-81 harvest, for instance, Baby

'Operation Parsley'

'But in September 1937, crisis was at the door, in fact was already in. Trujillo had made promises to his people that he couldn't keep, that is, if he ever had any intention of doing so. Fiscal resources were running dangerously low. The axe was not long in falling.

"It's the immigrants' fault", rumbled the rumor, carefully nourished, as always in such cases, by the authorities and the media. "It's the Haitians! They must be driven out."

His excellence the Generalissimo Dr Raphael Trujillo Molina, honorable President of the Republic, Benefactor of the Fatherland and Reconstructor of Financial Independence, summed up the situation in a few words which evoked the admiration of all the brown-nosers in his entourage: "*these are foreign negroes in our country; contemptible livestock thieves, practitioners of voodoo. Their presence in our territory can only deteriorate the living conditions of our citizens.*"

There was really nothing to add, and no one added anything, except the press, which launched a virulent anti-Haitian public opinion campaign.

No one ever really confirmed that the fatal order was given in the course of a drinking bout one night, in which Trujillo wanted to please one of his mistresses who was irritated by the presence of the black workers in the countryside. But no one ever really refuted it. Anyway, what is certain, and the rest is of little importance, is that the order was given, and given good.

[Ti-Jacques] was walking in the countryside, drowned in sun and fierce heat, holding little Marcel by the hand, when three individuals accosted him, three guys looking grim and determined. Eyebrows raised, they had stopped him. The smallest was holding in his hand what appeared to be at first sight the leaf of some green plant, and he held it out in the direction of Ti-Jacques.

"*Hola hombre, cómo se llama esa cosa?* Tell me, what is this thing called?"

Ti-Jacques had looked at it, astonished. Funny question.

"Why, it's *pe'sil* (parsley), of course!"

Exactly what they were hoping. The three were not peasants, but Trujillo's soldiers in disguise.

A Haitian, even when he can speak Spanish well, which was the case with Ti-Jacques, experiences serious difficulties in pronouncing it. He has an especially hard time with the "r" and the "j". As for articulating the word parsley, *perejil*, obstructed with "r" and "j", which rolls on the tongue, and scrapes the back of the throat, that one is practically impossible. *Perejil* becomes pe'ejil, or pe'e'il, or yet pe'e'i, but never, ever, *perejil*.

"It's pe'sil, of course!"

"You are a Haitian, you! A brigand, a bandit, a horse thief!"

"I am Haitian, Señor, but I never..."

He didn't have the leisure to explain that he had never stolen the slightest animal. That wasn't really the issue. In the border region, any black individual incapable of pronouncing the word *perejil* was henceforth a condemned man. Uncomprehending, little Marcel saw his father collapse, losing buckets

> of blood that seemed to never stop. His eyes opened wide, and his cry of
> terror was drowned in the flood of his own blood. He wasn't quite two
> years old, but that day, a Haitian was a Haitian. "Operation perejil" was in
> full swing.'
>
> (Lemoine 1985:134-5)

Doc's regime received US$2.9 million for supplying 16,000 Haitian workers (Veras 1983:56). According to Roger Plant (1987:117), the Haitian ambassador in Santo Domingo personally delivered US$2 million in suitcases to Duvalier in January 1986, a month before Baby Doc was overthrown.

The officially recruited workers were known as *kongos* and were supposed to work during the harvest period and then return to Haiti. Many, either through choice or simply because they had not earned any money, stayed in the Dominican Republic, swelling the numbers of the so-called *viejos* or old hands. These Haitians became more-or-less permanent residents, some marrying Dominican women, but very few received recognition as Dominican citizens. A third category of Haitian workers, known as the *ambafiles* (literally, 'below the wire') crossed the border illegally in search of work. Sometimes these Haitians were forced to bribe Dominican border guards and other officials in order to enter the country. Otherwise, the highly porous 300 kilometre border proved no great obstacle.

Most of these Haitians worked on the CEA plantations through agreements between the CEA and the Haitian Ministry of Social Affairs which in turn referred back to the 1966 contract between the Balaguer government and Papa Doc Duvalier. In theory, each worker was to receive certain minimum benefits and guaranteed facilities, such as acceptable accommodation, safe transportation, medical insurance and a basic wage for each ton of cane cut. In reality, few of these benefits ever materialised, and the *braceros* worked long hours for a pittance before returning to the squalor of the *batey*. Conditions on the private-sector Central Romana and Vicini estates were reputedly somewhat better. As a result, many Haitians tried to escape from the CEA plantations, but were often intercepted by troops or security guards and forcibly returned.

Forced Labour

The situation changed drastically in 1986 with the downfall of the 30-year Duvalier dictatorship. The end of the regime brought the end

'Sheer hell...'

'My findings, to those people familiar with the Haitians' situation, were perhaps nothing new; they served only to corroborate previous accounts of thousands of Haitian workers, often barefoot and clad in torn shirts, complaining of working from before dawn until the late evening for a pittance, well below their expectations, which allowed them the choice of returning without savings or half-starving for the six months of the harvest season. They gave endless accounts of threats and reprisals, of cheating over weights, of being compelled to work on rest days. When I tried to discuss the contents of the bilateral contract, I seemed to be wasting my time... In some of the *ingenios*, most notably in Gulf & Western's La Romana, there were indications that old *bateyes* had been modernised and new ones built in the course of the past few years. However, as I soon found out, these were never where the Kongos were required to live. Either at the end of the Dominican quarters, or in separate and more remote quarters set aside specifically for the Kongos, there were rudimentary concrete rooms, usually equipped with metal beds and sometimes with old mattresses, but nothing else. Dining rooms, bathrooms, running water, recreation centres? Even CEA officials laughed when I mentioned them. Haitians cooked outside on primitive wood fires, walked several hundred yards to collect water from an evil-looking spigot, as often as not had no toilets, and in the worst cases lived in primitive shacks with leaking roofs that must have been sheer hell when the rainy season began in early May.'

(Plant 1987:100)

of the inter-governmental contract and a consequent massive shortage of Haitian labour. The contracted *kongos* had, of course, never accounted for all the Haitian workforce, making up perhaps 15,000 out of an estimated total of 40,000 Haitians employed by the CEA. The other workers were mostly resident *viejos*, many living permanently on the *bateyes* and other Haitians, some illegal and others coerced.

There has always been evidence of coercion and forced labour in the Dominican sugar plantations. With the end of the contract, however, the critical labour shortage led to increasingly brutal measures from the Dominican authorities. These were outlined in a report published in October 1989 by the US-based human rights organisation, Americas Watch.

According to Americas Watch, Haitians were recruited in the following ways. Some were offered employment in Haiti by so-called *buscones* or scouts, usually Haitians themselves, who promised high

Batey accommodation at La Romana. (Philip Wolmuth)

wages and good conditions. Frequently, they pretended to be recruiting for different work altogether. The *buscones* would then lead their recruits to the border, where in towns such as Jimaní they would be arrested by the Dominican military and then taken forcibly to a CEA plantation. In return, the *buscón* received a per capita payment of about US$10. (By the 1990-91 harvest, this had risen to US$25 per head, due to the worsening labour shortage). Alternatively, Haitians were regularly picked up in roadblock searches or raids on certain communities by the military. These round-ups particularly affected *viejos* who might be working in some other economic sector (Americas Watch 1989:13-19).

The Americas Watch report raised a storm of controversy inside the Dominican Republic, where ministers dismissed it as inaccurate and malicious. It also focused international attention on the abuses occurring within the country. In particular, the US Trade Representative, empowered to cut any country's access to the US Generalized System of Preferences (GSP, preferential access to the US market), agreed to accept Americas Watch's petition and to review alleged abuses of labour rights in the Dominican Republic before extending Dominican eligibility to the GSP.

Stolen Childhood

'Batey Duqueza is also in Ingenio Rio Haina. In early February 1991, the Lawyers Committee interviewed five children who had recently arrived from Haiti to cut cane: Bernard Florial, 16 years old, Sainsain Charles, 15 years old, Juanex Calanche, 12 years old, Daniel Jean, 14 years old, and Sauver Charles, 8 years old. They were part of a group of 60 new recruits...who were turned over by a *buscone* called "Jauneru" to the CEA at the border town of Jimaní in November 1990. Each child said it was the first time they had ever cut cane and found the work hard and dangerous. They must work 12 hours a day, from 6am to 6pm. They do not go to school. They sleep 6 to a room; the Lawyers Committee examined the room where they sleep. The room is bare except for a few bent and rusty bunkbeds that have neither mattresses nor blankets. There is no electricity or running water. One boy was cooking his dinner of rice in front of the barracks in a pot over an open fire.

The boys stated that they are not free to leave the plantation. They added that they are even prohibited from leaving their rooms at night and must stay inside until 4am when they are allowed out to wash... They are paid with vouchers which they use in the store on the plantation to buy enough food to survive. The store takes 20% off the face value of the voucher, a common practice throughout the cane communities. The boys said they never see cash since they must buy food and cannot wait for the end of the two-week period to cash their vouchers.'

(Lawyers Committee for Human Rights 1991:6-7)

Having indignantly denied the main allegations of the Americas Watch report, the Dominican government then curiously began to introduce a number of reforms. In October 1990, Balaguer ordered the issue of individual contracts to Haitian cane-cutters, the regularisation of the immigration status of all Haitians in the country and improvements in conditions in the *bateyes*. A subsequent Americas Watch report, *Half Measures*, recognised a few improvements, but maintained that widespred abuses in recruitment and inhumane conditions persisted. Nonetheless, in May 1991 the US Trade Representative ruled against the Americas Watch petition and in favour of maintaining the Dominican Republic's trade benefits. The decision was based on reports from the US embassy in Santo Domingo that 'abuses of Haitian cane cutters appear to be much less widespread in this harvest season.' It should be noted that in the 1989 Americas

Watch report, the embassy official concerned with human rights policy admitted to never having seen a *batey*.

Another incriminating report, published by the US Lawyers Committee for Human Rights in May 1991, merely reinforced the evidence of widespread labour and human rights abuses. Specifically, it pointed out that an unknown number of children, some as young as six, are forced to work on the Dominican plantations. Of these some are illegally recruited by *buscones* in Haiti, while others grow up in the Dominican Republic, either on the *bateyes* or in other communities. Refused access to education, these children — along with other *braceros* — are regularly cheated of their due earnings, paid with vouchers (which they can only exchange in the over-priced *batey* store and prevented from leaving by armed guards.

Balaguer Hits Back

The barrage of criticism levelled against the Dominican government produced an unexpected result in June 1991, when Balaguer decreed the deportation of all illegal Haitian immigrants aged under 16 or over 60. The first group of 29 children who had been working on a sugar plantation were sent back to Haiti on 18 June, to be met at the frontier post of Malpasse by the Haitian Foreign Minister. Within three months, an estimated 50,000 Haitians had been deported or had left voluntarily to avoid being rounded up by Dominican troops. Further human rights reports alleged that Haitians were robbed by military personnel, beaten up and separated from their families. Some people of Haitian descent but born in the Dominican Republic were reportedly returned by force to a country they had never seen before. By mid-August, however, the pace of deportations had slowed.

The tit-for-tat nature of the deportation policy was evident in Balaguer's reported remark that his government had 'the right to treat the Haitians the same way as the United States or Puerto Rico treat Dominicans' (*Caribbean Insight* July 1991). Justifying his decree, he also referred to 'an unfair campaign from abroad', an allusion to the human rights reports and a much-publicised ABC television documentary about the *bateyes*.

The government response was widely supported within the Dominican Republic, and newspapers carried many articles and editorials attacking foreign interference in the country's economic affairs and developing the traditional theme of Dominican national identity. The time-honoured references to the 19th-century Haitian occupation and the neighbouring country's territorial ambitions resurfaced once more alongside the explicitly racist concepts of cultural invasion and biological degeneration. The racism of Balaguer's best-selling 1984 book, *La Isla a revés*, was again in vogue:

> The erosion of Dominican national identity, steadily under way for more than a century through dealings with the worst of the Haitian population, has made worrying advances. Our racial origins and our tradition as a Spanish people must not stop us from recognising that our nationality is in danger of disintegration if we do not take drastic measures against the threat to it from the proximity of the Haitian people... The first symptom of this loss of identity is the progressive ethnic decadence of the Dominican population... There are other signs, less obvious, but perhaps more dangerous, of Haiti's influence over the moral and physical makeup of the Dominican people. (Balaguer 1984:45)

Other anti-Haitian themes included allegations that food smuggling from the Dominican Republic into Haiti was causing shortages and that Haitian immigrants were responsible for the growing incidence of AIDS. In May 1991, a group called the National Defence Organisation announced it would be leading demonstrations against the Haitian presence in the country.

Beyond the Bateyes

Not all Dominicans took part in the anti-Haitian campaign. The general manager of the CEA, Juan Arturo Biaggi, complained, for instance, that bona fide *braceros* were being rounded up or intimidated into returning to Haiti, exacerbating the labour shortage during the harvest period. He also pointed out at a press conference that of an official estimate of 500,000 Haitians resident in the Dominican Republic, only three per cent were engaged in the sugar industry. Other Dominican industrialists and landowners also opposed the measure, fearful of losing access to a supply of cheap and easily dispensable labour.

The campaign against human rights abuses in the *bateyes* had indeed served to obscure the fact that the Haitians living in the *bateyes* were merely the most visible sector of a much larger and diversified Haitian presence in the country. This presence, has become all the more conspicuous since the early 1980s, when the US government began to turn back the Haitian boatpeople who were attempting to sail to Florida in search of a better life.

Haitians work in all other sectors of agriculture, picking coffee, rice, tobacco and the new export crops destined for the US market. They also work in the construction industry, providing cheap labour for the government's programme of urban 'beautification' in Santo Domingo. When the building of the controversial Columbus lighthouse was at its height, it was possible to see hundreds of Haitians carrying concrete blocks into the edifice, as if labouring in the construction of a Pharoah's pyramid. Above all, Haitians are active in the country's informal sector, in the vast network of trading and services — legal and illegal — which provides a livelihood for increasing numbers of people (CRESDIP 1991:76).

The deportation decree threatened many of these resident Haitians and put further pressures on the already vulnerable government of Jean-Bertrand Aristide. When the coup d'etat of 29-30 September 1991 overthrew Aristide it came only days after the Haitian president had condemned the traditional slavery inflicted on *braceros* in the Dominican Republic during a speech to the UN General Assembly. The Balaguer government's refusal to condemn the coup was widely interpreted as proof of its hostility towards the radical Aristide and his outspoken criticism of conditions for Haitians in the Dominican Republic.

The repatriation decree, and the coup, also put paid, temporarily at least, to joint Dominican and Haitian government attempts to obtain European Community funding for common projects in infrastructure, manufacturing and tourism. Most importantly for Balaguer, however, the Haitian crisis created a timely distraction from the controversy surrounding renewed negotiations with the IMF (see chapter 6). It remains to be seen whether the 1991 anti-Haitian campaign has any long-term impact on the complex economic and cultural relationship between the two countries. In the ensuing debate there has been renewed talk of 'Dominicanising' the sugar industry by radically improving pay and conditions in order to attract a national workforce. PRD leader Peña Gómez, under attack for his allegedly Haitian origins and sympathies, has been an advocate of such measures and has emphasised the need to work constructively with Port-au-Prince. In the context of the Lomé agreement and European Community support for joint development projects, several prominent Dominican industrialists have urged cooperation with the Haitian government, stressing also that the Haitian population is the natural market for Dominican goods. An open letter of support for President Aristide, signed by several hundred Dominican intellectuals in October 1991, was further evidence of positive attitudes towards Haiti in Santo Domingo.

Yet, against this constructive outlook stands the accumulated prejudice and hatred of two centuries and an ingrained anti-Haitian instinct which runs through every sector of Dominican society. This instinct is easily played upon by Dominican politicians for their own purposes and creates a convenient mythology of national solidarity. It is by no means clear, however, whether this mythology can withstand the economic crisis and the new realities of the 1990s.

6

Pain and Protest

On Monday 23 April 1984 Santo Domingo erupted. Following the relative tranquillity of the Easter weekend, a sudden wave of popular protest and fury shook the capital. Its immediate cause was a series of dramatic price rises, announced by the government the previous Thursday and introduced that morning in the country's shops. Medicines went up by 200 per cent; rice, milk and cooking oil all doubled in price.

In the poverty-stricken *barrio* of Capotillo, 100 neighbourhood organisations had agreed a common programme of demands to President Jorge Blanco and the PRD government. They wanted the withdrawal of the price increases, a minimum monthly salary of 200 *pesos*, the provision of electricity and water to Capotillo residents and the abrogation of the agreement recently signed between the Dominican government and the International Monetary Fund. The organisers planned a twelve-hour strike, and shops, businesses and transport duly closed down altogether. As crowds gathered on the streets to demonstrate against the price rises the military went into action with batons and tear gas. The crowds fought back, erecting burning barricades and looting the local INESPRE distribution centre.

As riots spread throughout the capital and thirty other towns and villages, the troops opened fire. By 25 April, 112 Dominican civilians were dead (of whom 27 were women and 5 children), 500 more were wounded and 5,000 were under arrest. Of the dead and wounded nearly all were shot by the security forces. That day President Jorge Blanco publicly praised the military for its efforts:

> The armed forces and the National Police have given an example of restraint [*ecuanimidad*], displaying their high degree of professionalism, elevated human feeling and respect for life...

they have kept their reactions within the limits of reasonable prudence and displayed excellent training.

The riots of April 1984 finally destroyed the already flagging popularity of the PRD government and brought to the world's attention the social cost of the so-called stabilisation programmes which the IMF imposes upon indebted Third World countries. They also galvanised the Dominican popular movement which since the early 1980s has posed the most fundamental challenge to the country's old political order.

Condemned to Debt

By early 1983 the Dominican economy had reached the point of no return. Like almost every other country in Latin America, it was hopelessly in debt and unable to meet repayment obligations on existing loans. From a figure of US$600 million in 1973 the external debt had escalated to US$2,400 million ten years later. The debt crisis was in many ways the hangover which followed the euphoria of the short-lived 'Dominican miracle'. During the boom years of the early 1970s credit had been all too easily available. Encouraged by high commodity prices and a buoyant US economy, domestic businesses borrowed freely from the state-controlled Central Bank, often at subsidised rates. The Central Bank, in return, borrowed from US and European banks keen to recycle the so-called 'petrodollars' which the 1973-4 oil price rise had brought into the world banking system. Partly buffered against the first oil shock by the high sugar price of 1974 and foreign investment, the Dominican economy, with its rapid industrialisation and construction boom, grew dramatically — but on credit.

The Balaguer government of 1966-78 was profligate, pushing up the debt from US$158 million in 1966 to US$1,100 million in 1977. Not only did it borrow heavily to complete its ambitious public works programme, but it also took large amounts of food from the US on credit which it distributed on subsidised terms to the poorest social sectors while at the same time holding down their wages. Between 1973 and 1983, over US$358 million of food was imported on mostly 20-year repayment schedules (Plant 1987:142). At the same time, Balaguer allowed the decentralised state corporations to contract their own loans from any available source. The economic elite did well out of these policies. Middle-class Santo Domingo was largely built during this period, while the elite spirited US$368 million out of the country and deposited it in private bank accounts abroad.

By the mid-1970s, the miracle was already running out of steam. Commodity prices dropped after the high point of 1974, the first oil price rise began to be felt in the state-sector industries and Balaguer's policy of holding down wages depressed those industries which catered to the domestic market. Meanwhile, the foreign companies which invested so spectacularly in the early 1970s withdrew their profits as the boom subsided. Between 1975 and 1978 for every dollar of new foreign investment, US$1.60 left the Dominican Republic as repatriated profit.

The PRD government which took power in 1978 inherited a sick economy. It also ran into a series of external shocks which exacerbated the crisis. World market prices for sugar, coffee and nickel were all in decline. Then, in August 1979, Hurricane David destroyed large areas of the Dominican Republic, killing some 1,000 people and causing approximately US$1,000 million in damage. It came one month after the second worldwide rise in oil prices which inflated the country's import bill and precipitated recession in the US and a resulting rise in world interest rates. As exports dropped and interest rates rose, debt servicing climbed from US$87 million in 1978 to US$250 million in 1982. That year, the world sugar price stood at a mere five cents per pound, as opposed to 76 cents per pound in 1975.

Squeezed by external forces, the Guzmán administration tried to honour its election pledge to reduce unemployment by resorting to the time-honoured strategy of massive public-sector recruitment. Within two years it created 60,000 jobs, mostly for PRD loyalists. Guzmán also raised the minimum wage and decreed a ten per cent wage rise to public-sector workers, the first for several years. To increase its popularity further, the PRD government encouraged the CDE and INESPRE to provide the urban poor with cheap electricity and subsidised food. To finance these measures, Guzmán was forced to borrow more and to print money, thereby fuelling inflation.

Following Guzmán's suicide in July 1982, Jorge Blanco took office for a further four-year PRD term and found the state coffers empty. The balance of payments deficit for that year stood at US$560 million, while the Central Bank, starved of reserves, owed US$200 million in overdue debt repayments. The new PRD government promised an 'economic democracy'; it introduced a programme of moderate tax increases and banned some luxury imports to preserve hard currency. But confidence in the PRD's economic management was fading fast. Guzmán's nationalisation of a single US enterprise, the Rosario Dominicano goldmine, in 1979 had already disturbed US investors. The *peso*, although officially worth one dollar, was losing its value as Dominicans preferred to put their trust in dollars, and by 1982 the dollar had risen to 1.35 *pesos* on the parallel market.

Jorge Blanco had to face the inevitable. Only an agreement with the IMF would give the Dominican government access to new funds. But these new funds were only available at a heavy social cost.

The IMF

On 21 January 1983 the PRD administration reached agreement with the IMF on a a three-year extended loan facility, worth US$466 million. The first US$195.8 million was to be made available that year, with the next installment to be renegotiated the following January. The agreement's importance to the Dominican government went beyond the actual money involved, since the IMF's seal of approval for the government's policies was a precondition for renegotiating existing debts and gaining access to fresh loans. The conditions attached to the IMF's support, however, were stringent. As elsewhere in the Third World, the multilateral agency insisted on a sweeping 'stabilisation' programme, aiming to cut government spending and increase export earnings as a way of paying back the debt. In the first year the IMF insisted that the government honour overdue debt repayments, reduce Central Bank loans to the public sector, freeze state-sector salaries and remove most import restrictions. Most importantly, it stipulated that the Dominican *peso* — which since 1947 had been officially fixed at par with the dollar — should be devalued by officially recognising the existing parallel or black market exchange rate and creating a single rate based on the *peso*'s real value.

Devaluation of the *peso* involved more than a psychological blow to Dominican national pride. It meant that the price of imports, held down by an artificially high *peso*, would rise dramatically, while exports would become much more competitive. For the PRD government, it was a choice between hurting domestic consumers and boosting exports by devaluation or protecting domestic consumption and stifling exports by maintaining an overvalued *peso*. The IMF favoured the former as a way of redressing the balance of payments imbalance; the government realised, however, that to raise the price of imported goods too steeply would spell political disaster. This was especially the case since so many basic items — food, oil, medicines — are imported into the Dominican Republic.

Jorge Blanco tried to compromise. The government maintained dollar-*peso* parity for imports of oil and medicines (thereby effectively subsidising these items) but allowed basic foods to rise according to free-market pressures. Protests broke out at once, as milk, eggs, wheat and other staples rose in price. The IMF, however, was not satisfied, and at the end of the first year insisted that the parallel exchange rate

The shantytown area of Santa Barbara in Santo Domingo: due for demolition in the beautification scheme. (Philip Wolmuth)

would have to be eliminated altogether as a pre-condition for receiving the second installment. In the meantime, it refused to pay any more to the Dominican Republic and effectively blocked loans and grants from other quarters.

The PRD government now blamed the IMF for all its economic woes and appealed in an open letter to President Reagan to intercede on its behalf. Reagan advised the Dominicans to bow to the IMF's demands and USAID froze the 1984 US$80 million aid package until this was done. After a series of desperate meetings, Jorge Blanco was forced to capitulate. On 19 April he announced that food and medicine prices would be liberalised. Four days later the riots began. Far from signalling the end of the IMF 'stabilisation' programme, the 1984 unrest was followed by further, more sweeping economic reforms. By mid-1985, after yet another package of austerity measures, the *peso* was floating at a market rate of 3.30 to the dollar, with all imports being paid for at that rate. The IMF had also forced Jorge Blanco to reduce the government subsidy on imported oil, thereby passing on price increases to consumers. By the beginning of 1985, food prices had already increased by an average of 50 to 100 per cent over the previous year. As a result, *Caribbean Insight* reported in June 1985, poor families in Santo Domingo could no longer afford meat, milk or even plantains — normally a cheap Caribbean staple.

Moreover, as it decreed price rises, the government systematically held down wages and repressed popular protest. In February 1985 the government responded to protests and a general strike by arresting hundreds of trade unionists and shooting four demonstrators. Armed soldiers surrounded the house of Juan Bosch.

Despite the enormous cost to poor Dominicans, it is debatable whether the IMF-approved policies really improved the Dominican economy. Certain sectors certainly profited handsomely from the devaluation, most notably foreign and domestic entrepreneurs with interests in export-led industries and tourism. For them, the devaluation meant dramatically reduced labour costs in dollar terms and a huge increase in their *peso* earnings from exports abroad. But for the ailing state-sector industries such as sugar, power, and basic foods, the austerity programme was disastrous, exposing them to sudden price rises in imported fuel and machinery. The outcome, predictably, was inflation — from 4.8 per cent in 1983 to 37.5 per cent in 1985. Between 1980 and 1985 the real value of the minimum wage fell by 20 per cent. As Deere *et al* (1990:43) point out:

> rather than the stability promised by IMF technicians, the Dominican Republic has seen increased inflation and unemployment and negative GDP growth rates. Measured unemployment increased from 21 per cent in 1981 to 27 per cent in 1985. Even though foreign investment in the export-processing zones boomed in the 1980s, gross domestic investment was negative between 1980 and 1985, recovering only in 1986. The main accomplishment of this austerity program was that the Dominican Republic was able to meet its debt-servicing commitments — $571 million, amounting to 76 per cent of export earnings, was repaid in 1985 — and the country's external debt was rescheduled thanks to the 'good offices' of the IMF.

The Crisis Continues

The IMF played a large part in the PRD's electoral defeat of 1986 and in the return of Joaquín Balaguer. Balaguer had witnessed what the IMF had done to the PRD's popularity and at first distanced himself from dealing with the agency. In any case, his initial economic plans were hardly compatible with the IMF prescription of budgetary restraint and austerity. Instead, Balaguer proposed to revitalise the economy through a massive programme of public works, aimed at creating jobs and boosting related economic sectors. In 1988 and 1989, the Balaguer regime spent more in capital expenditure (in other words, the building programme) than on current expenditure such as salaries. As a result, wages were further cut back, while imports related to the construction boom forced up inflation. In 1989 inflation stood at 45 per cent; in 1990 it approached 100 per cent before recessionary policies forced it down again.

In 1990 Balaguer adopted a radically different economic approach, cutting back public spending and capital investment by almost 50 per cent. The attempt to stop inflation appeared to have succeeded by the end of 1991, when the rate fell from 100 per cent to single figures. But this was achieved at the cost of a severe recession, with GDP falling by 5.1 per cent in 1990 and a forecast five per cent again in 1991. The construction industry which had boomed in the previous four years was particularly badly hit, with widescale job losses.

The *peso*, meanwhile, steadily lost its value, slipping from the official rate of 3.30 to the dollar in 1985 to a parallel market rate of 7.90 in June 1988. In August the government forcibly closed down the private *casas de cambio* and insisted that all foreign exchange transactions be conducted through commercial banks under Central Bank supervision at a single 6.35 rate. The pressure to devalue further and a booming black market took the *peso* to 10.20 per dollar in 1990 and 12.67 by the end of 1991.

Nor did the Dominican debt crisis improve with Balaguer's return. Although Jorge Blanco's austerity programme had persuaded commercial banks to reschedule US$765 million of debt in 1986, by early 1987 the debt had risen to US$4,200 million. In 1990, the US embassy in Santo Domingo reported that the Dominican government had interest arrears of more than US$700 million and owed a total sum equivalent to 75 per cent of GDP. Of this, it owed 22 per cent to commercial banks, 34 per cent to the so-called Paris Club of developed country government lenders, 15 per cent to other bilateral lenders (chiefly Mexico and Venezuela for oil supplies), 26 per cent to international institutions (the IMF, World Bank, IADB) and three per cent to short-term suppliers.

Another agreement with the IMF seemed increasingly inevitable, despite Balaguer's repeated refusals to follow the PRD's example. After several years of rumour and counter-rumour, Balaguer finally announced in June 1991 that the IMF would provide an 18-month standby facility of US$113 million. More importantly, the pact provided for the renegotiation of US$926 million in debt to the Paris Club. The IMF's conditions were as follows: market-led adjustment of the dollar-*peso* exchange rate, the payment of debt arrears, an end to subsidies to state corporations and the elimination of price controls. The agreement signalled an important change in Balaguer's attitude towards the debt problem, and the government began to catch up with the payment of arrears. Again it was a recipe that would do most harm to the poor.

Growing Poverty

Inflation, devaluation and tough incomes policies have made the Dominican poor much poorer in the course of the 1980s. The Central Bank estimates that in that decade the real value of average wages fell by 32.5 per cent. In October 1989, for example, the minimum monthly salary was established at 650 *pesos*. At the prevailing dollar exchange rate of 6.28 *pesos*, this was worth US$103.50. Yet although the minimum wage was raised in September 1990 to 1,040 *pesos*, devaluation had reduced the *peso* to 10.20 to the dollar, giving a real monthly salary of only US$101.96. According to the Economic Research Centre, 57 per cent of Dominicans now live in poverty, up from 47 per cent in 1984, while 30 per cent live in absolute poverty, compared to 16 per cent in 1984. The gap between rich and poor has also widened; in 1991 20 per cent of households accounted for 61 per cent of income, while the poorest 20 per cent shared less than three per cent.

Fiscal policy particularly benefits the wealthy and hurts the poor. Income tax is extremely low and is often simply avoided by the rich through political favouritism, special exemptions and fraud. Excise tax on alcoholic beverages actually raises more revenue than total national income tax (Cuddington and Asilis 1990:349). The main source of revenue, however, is import and export taxes. The former push up the price of many imported staple foods and domestic goods, while the latter take a large cut from the income of small peasant producers who cultivate such export crops as coffee, tobacco and cocoa. The multinational export industries which operate inside the IFZs, however, rarely pay any tax whatsoever, enjoying exemptions from both import and export taxation. Attempts to introduce a redistributive system of income and property taxation have met with predictable hostility from the economic elite. Juan Bosch's proposals for moderate fiscal reform played an important role in his downfall.

The government's recurring fiscal deficit, caused largely by inadequate tax collection, as well as the debt crisis, means that social services, theoretically provided by right in the Dominican Constitution, are increasingly under strain. Spending on education, for instance, fell from 13.3 per cent of the government budget in 1983 to 6.7 per cent in 1988. This halving of resources means larger classes, fewer qualified teachers, dilapidated buildings and massive levels of non-attendance among children from poor families. An estimated 80 per cent of teachers receive less than the national minimum wage. Although education is nominally free and compulsory for all children between seven and 14, it is estimated that 66 per cent of children attending primary school do not complete their education. With a rapidly rising birthrate (official government figures suggest that 39

Debt Crisis, Birth Crisis

'Formally speaking, access to health care remains free. Patients, however, are required to provide their own bed linens and medicines. Furthermore, women who plan to deliver their babies at public hospitals are told to buy whatever supplies they need at the local pharmacy and to bring those supplies to the hospital with them. These include the xylocaine, pitocin, and sterile gloves commonly used during labor and delivery. Immediately after delivery, women and their newborn infants are wheeled into a recovery room and placed in a bed where they remain for the following 12 to 24 hours until they are discharged. Often they share the bed with another woman and her infant. Frequently neither woman can supply a sheet or pillow, so they lie feet-to-head on plastic mattresses. And more often than not, there is no running water with which to wash, forcing women to spend their recovery time lying in their own blood.'
(Whiteford 1991:8)

per cent of the population is under 15), the crisis in education is doing long-term damage to the country's future. But for the part played by various Church organisations in teaching at all levels, the situation would be even worse. Meanwhile, private establishments cater for the children of the wealthy in Santo Domingo, preparing them for training at North American universities.

Health services, which underwent considerable expansion and improvement in the 1960s and 1970s, are also chronically under-resourced and inadequate. Preventable illnesses such as tuberculosis and typhoid, spread through poor sanitation, polluted water and substandard housing, have begun to increase in the late 1980s and early 1990s, with significant outbreaks of typhoid in the Santo Domingo slum area of La Ciénaga ('the swamp') in the summers of 1990 and 1991. In the second epidemic an estimated 30 children died. Public hospitals lack the most basic drugs and equipment, while continual power cuts add to the difficulties of providing treatment. Vaccination programmes are inadequate; in 1991 only 52 per cent of children under the age of one were vaccinated against preventable diseases. Like teachers, medical staff are underpaid, leading to massive emigration among qualified doctors and nurses and general demoralisation. In the first part of 1991, medical workers were among the most militant in their opposition to Balaguer's austerity policies. In August, 7,000 doctors finally ended a 12-week strike after the government agreed to raise their salaries by 50 per cent.

Despite the seemingly endless construction activity around Santo Domingo, most Dominicans face poor housing conditions and basic services. In 1989, for instance, 63 per cent of the population had no access to electricity. According to the daily newspaper, *Listín Diario*, in 1990 seven out of ten families had no sanitary facilities in their homes; eight out of ten had no piped water, while 40 per cent of water consumed was believed polluted. According to UNICEF, almost 60,000 Dominican children live permanently on the streets. Refuse collection in many urban areas is almost non-existent, forcing people to dump rubbish in populated areas, increasing the risk of disease. Even the elegant middle-class districts of Santo Domingo are blighted by foul-smelling heaps of rubbish left uncollected in the streets.

The Popular Movement

In the shantytown *barrio* of La Ciénaga the shacks of wood and corrugated iron tumble down to the dirty water of the Ozama river. When it rains and the river rises, houses are flooded or even swept away. Because there is no refuse collection, people have thrown their rubbish into gulleys and pathways. A damaged wall in the *barrio*'s main drainage channel has made the problem worse, threatening the inhabitants with sudden flooding when tropical storms send torrents of water down the steep hillside.

With the financial help of international aid agencies, the Neighbourhood Rights Defence Committee (COPADEBA) is reconstructing the broken wall. Local people do the work. At the same time, COPADEBA is setting up a number of 'popular shops' in the most deprived urban areas, where basic foods will be bought in bulk and sold at no profit to local people. But the organisation's main task is to campaign against the forced evictions of slum dwellers who stand in the way of the Balaguer government's 'beautification' scheme.

Founded in 1979 as a response to the power of large landowners in the growing slum areas, COPADEBA is now the biggest popular organisation in Santo Domingo. Its roots lie within the radical Catholic Church, but its rank-and-file membership is overwhelmingly made up of ordinary inhabitants of the slum districts. A series of local committees, regularly elected, sends delegates to a regional committee which coordinates policy and action. An estimated 87 per cent of COPADEBA's membership is made up of women.

The Dominican popular movement, like its equivalents in other Latin American countries, grew in strength due to the economic crisis of the 1980s and the resulting deterioration in social conditions. It also reflects the same region-wide disenchantment with traditional party politics

'We started with a bag of rice'

'I work in a school and do washing at weekends, and sometimes in the afternoons I fry snacks for people. I sell fried plantain, cheap bits of chicken like legs, liver and neck, cornflour bread, sweet potato and spaghetti. I manage....

I also work in a neighbourhood organisation. When I finish my work I go around inviting people to meetings. When we have a meeting or have to go somewhere I don't go to work. I stop doing whatever I have to. The organisational work takes precedence...

Through the organisation we have achieved what we talked about earlier, the wall for the waste gutter which was a very big problem. We had this work done and organised the people in the *barrio* who didn't know what to do. And we have a community shop where we can get cheaper food, which is a big help. We started with a sack of rice and a tin of oil and now we can buy larger quantities, ten or more sacks and tins of oil and lots of other things, and we want to increase the range of food we sell...

Services are very few or practically non-existent. We don't have any refuse collection. That's why we had that problem with the waste gutter. That is where the people throw away their rubbish. There is no other place to throw it. We are working on the water situation. It is very scarce. You have to go a long way to fetch it, so we are trying to solve that problem. Down here we don't have a school, so children have to go up the hill and it's very dangerous for little children. It's not possible for us to take them to school because we have to work. So they have to go on their own or rely on some passer-by to help them cross the road...

We don't have any hospitals. There is a medical dispensary at the Domingo Sabio church... In the 17th Street there is a private clinic... You can only go to the private clinic if you have 40 *pesos*...

Sometimes I feel desperate. I think I work so hard and I don't seem to get anywhere. I always pray to God to give me strength, which is very important for me. That helps me a lot and gives me hope that we can change this situation, working of course, but at least with the hope of being able to change things.'

Interview with Basilia Rulesindo, local COPADEBA coordinator, Santo Domingo

Source: Oxfam

---

as a means of achieving concrete improvements in everyday living conditions. Through their experience of the corruption, clientilism and incompetence attached to the party political system, many Dominicans are alienated from the electoral process and expect little from politicians. As a result, popular protest often takes alternative forms, even though political parties attempt to harness such protest to their own objectives.

It was the PRD governments of 1978-86 and their relative liberalisation of Dominican society which allowed political activity, and the popular organisations, to grow more freely after the repression of the 1966-78 Balaguer regime. During that period there had been influential organisations such as mothers' clubs and youth and sports' associations, but their militancy had been much curtailed by the persecution of political activists. When the PRD came to power in 1978, however, as during the ephemeral Bosch presidency, trade unions, peasant groups, Church-led organisations, student bodies, left-wing parties and neighbourhood committees proliferated. The trade union movement, in particular, experienced a new sense of freedom after the coercion and restrictive legislation of the Balaguer years. New unions and confederations appeared, while the political parties, the PRD, the PLD, the Communist Party and far-left groups struggled for influence within them. At the same time, the schism between the highly conservative hierarchy of the Dominican Catholic Church and its radical grassroots activists widened. In slum districts and impoverished rural backwaters, a new generation of priests was instrumental in forming *comunidades de base* (base communities) which combined liberation theology with practical economic development projects.

From these various currents within Dominican society emerged a heterogeneous popular movement. To some extent, it owed its existence, character and strategies to the weaknesses of other organisations. The trade unions, for example, were hopelessly fragmented and open to political cooption; they also represented a small percentage of Dominican workers (today only 12 per cent of the workforce is unionised) and had neither the strength nor resources to carry out effective industrial action. Left-wing parties, with their tendency towards sectarian divisions and splits, also failed to create a credible opposition to the main parties.

More importantly, the popular movement was, and is, made up primarily of people traditionally excluded from conventional political organisations: women, youth, the unemployed, the marginalised workers of the so-called informal sector. These workers, who earn a living as domestic servants, street sellers or in thousands of small workshops and small businesses, belong to no trade union and may have little day-to-day contact with the established political parties. The movement has no single national leadership or structure (although attempts have been made to create these), but is based on communities and neighbourhoods. Its objectives are consequently local in form and concrete: access to piped water or electricity, the construction of a school or medical clinic, the creation of a communal credit system or neighbourhood shop.

The Santo Domingo-based research centre, CEDEE, records and analyses the actions undertaken by the popular movement and its different objectives on a six-monthly basis. Between January and June 1990, for instance, CEDEE monitored 102 different actions. Of these 20 were in support of increased wages, 20 for land titles, nine for improvements to local health services and nine for the provision of housing. The rest covered such issues as increased flour prices, a community made homeless by a mining scheme and general working conditions.

Objectives such as these invariably bring popular organisations into conflict with the state. Sometimes, popular pressure can bring results, especially around election time when political parties are more inclined to listen to their potential voters. But more often than not, demands for improved social services are ignored. The traditional strategy of the popular movement, the neighbourhood strike, often leads to physical confrontation with the police and other security forces as protestors try to block roads in order to bring a neighbourhood literally to a standstill. But over the years, organisers of such strikes have grown adept at avoiding head-on clashes with the police. Coordination between different neighbourhoods and regions also means that the security forces are faced with many simultaneous demonstrations. According to CEDEE, the range of popular actions includes local stoppages, workplace strikes, land seizures, demonstrations, pickets and the occupation of local government buildings.

The IMF riots of 1984 marked the areas where the popular movement was to be most active in the following years. The most militant organisations have grown up in slum areas of Santo Domingo such as Capotillo and La Ciénaga and in other cities such as San Pedro Macorís and Santiago. These are the urban districts which have grown disproportionately through migration from the countryside since the 1960s. As a result, they suffer a critical shortage of basic services and amenities. Since 1984, these and other districts have witnessed a succession of actions in support of specific local demands.

In the rural areas there is less of a tradition of militancy, although a strong sense of community solidarity often exists. This has led sociologists to contrast urban unrest with the *pobreza tranquila* (peaceful poverty) of the countryside. Yet, the late 1970s witnessed an increase in peasant organisation and activity, particularly centred around the fight for agrarian reform. In 1979 the Independent Peasant Movement (MCI) was founded, which by 1985 claimed a membership of 75,000. Radical in its campaigns for land redistribution and improved prices

'Let's fight for better services, health, education and food': popular
demonstration in Santo Domingo *barrio*, 1991.   (Julio Etchart)

and services, the MCI has also raised more general political issues
such as the debt crisis and the government's relationship with the IMF.

Beyond local strikes, demonstrations and land occupations, the
popular organisations have regularly come together to carry out
nationwide protests. In March 1988, for instance, the National
Conference of Popular Organisations, a national network of local
groups, called for a 48-hour general strike in protest at food price rises.
The strike was only partly successful and was abandoned after one
day. In June 1989, however, a better organised 48-hour strike,
supported by 307 trade union and popular groups, completely stopped
all activity in the country. Its demands, ignored by the Balaguer
government, were explicitly national and political: an increased
minimum wage, an end to debt repayments and specific economic and
agrarian reforms.

The 'New Actors'

The popular organisations have succeeded because they are different
from the established political parties. Whereas these are hierarchical,
authoritarian and male-dominated, the popular movement is
characterised by democratic participation and the widescale

involvement of women. The National Confederation of Peasant Women (CONAMUCA), for example, has a membership of 8,000 drawn from 21 regional federations. It works alongside the MCI, but at the same time retains its independence from what it sees as a machismo-dominated organisation. A survey of women's participation in Santo Domingo in 1989 revealed that 17 intermediate organisations and 39 base groups were exclusively involved with women's popular education and action (Ianni 1990:88). For many women the popular organisations offer a way to address the problems they encounter on a daily basis.

But this emphasis on local problems has brought criticism, notably from the traditional left-wing parties, that the popular organisations have no coherent long-term strategy. Critics have also accused *barrio* organisations of relieving the state of its social responsibilities, of establishing a parallel structure of social services which replaces what the state fails to provide. When political activists have tried to take over the popular organisations there has been considerable friction. After the spectacular militancy of 1984, for instance, a series of Popular Struggle Committees (CLPs) were established in order to coordinate protest action nationally. Attempts by political groups to take control of the CLPs led to disagreements and splits, with the formation of rival and parallel organisations. In late 1991 there were two main coordinating bodies: the CLPs and the more powerful Collective of Popular Organisations (COP). The COP led a number of local disputes in 1991 and organised a two-day national strike in July.

The popular movement is capable of mobilising large numbers of Dominicans to protest against government policy. However, it seems incapable of sustaining a united front and is prone to schisms and splits. Its very diversity and spontaneity work against a long-term political programme, while attempts to forge such a programme lead to divisions and leadership crises. As the sociologist Vanna Ianni (1990:91) concludes:

> The mass of the poor is not just the sum total of millions of isolated, atomised, alienated individuals. Instead, a dense network of interrelations binds together their daily lives; it unites and mixes kinship relationships with those between neighbours, work relationships with those built on common interests. Primary loyalties are interwoven with ties of mutual aid and become mixed up with the relations connected with various forms of *asociacionismo*. Neighbourhood committees, base Christian communities, housewives' committees, cultural and religious groups, sports clubs, parents' and school associations, environmental groups and, at an intermediate level, a plethora

of different organisations and institutions feed the permanent ebb and flow of interrelationships in town and countryside.

This is what determines popular feelings and perceptions; this network collects experiences and lived realities, links people's expectations and makes sense of their anxieties, fears and hopes. The unfolding of this web of interrelationships explains how the crisis of April 1984 came about and the events which followed. It also explains the repeated and deep difficulties which beset attempts to establish coordination of the different organisations, either at a national level or throughout the capital.

The central paradox of the popular movement is that it wields enormous political power but has so far been unwilling and unable to use that power within the established political system. It has no electoral ambitions, nor does it envisage a revolutionary seizure of power. Instead, it articulates the daily needs and aspirations of those who have been most clearly failed by the political system.

Conscious of these self-imposed limitations, some organisations within the popular movement have tried to formulate an explicitly political programme which goes beyond short-term single issues. The Research Group for Community Action (GRIPAC), for example, published a pamphlet in 1990 which called for the formation of a 'political, social and popular front'. According to GRIPAC:

As regards its *programme*, the political, social and popular front must take up those demands which have not yet been met in the last 499 years. Among these we can emphasise:

1. An end to the government's current economic policy and the resignation of Balaguer.
2. An increase in democracy, through political, constitutional, institutional, economic and social reforms.
3. The promotion of our cultural identity against foreign penetration.
4. The struggle for full national sovereignty and independence.
5. A coherent policy of national development which protects the world's environment.
6. The non-payment of the external debt, rejecting the IMF's stabilisation policies and supporting the establishment of a new international economic order.
7. A sovereign foreign policy which, recognising the right of peoples to self-determination, promotes solidarity and integration in the Caribbean, Latin America, and among the oppressed in all parts of the world.

8.   The establishment of a democratic and popular government.
     (GRIPAC 1990:21-2)

Alongside the organisations of the *barrios* and rural districts, professional associations, representing workers in the field of education, medicine, law and science, have also emerged in protest at declining social conditions. These qualified, middle-class professionals have been hit both by public-sector wage austerity and by spending cuts in schools, universities and hospitals. As a result, organisations such as the Dominican Medical Association (AMD) and the Dominican Teachers' Association (ADP) have come into bitter conflict with the government. The ADP, for instance, claiming that most state school teachers were earning only 550 *pesos* (US$44) per month, went on strike for three months in the summer of 1991. This action took place at the same time as doctors and nurses operated a go-slow in public hospitals.

The Dominican trade union movement, traditionally weak and divided, also underwent a process of revitalisation in the course of 1991. In May of that year, unions affiliated to the PLD, PRD and left-wing parties came together to form the United Confederation of Workers (CUT). Although still numerically weak, the CUT nevertheless marked a new departure for the Dominican labour movement. Its first confrontation with the Balaguer government came in July 1991, when it called a three-day general strike to demand a doubling of the minimum wage. The strike was abandoned on the second day, however, despite support from the two main opposition parties.

The almost permanent series of strikes against government economic policy produced only isolated concessions during the course of 1991. The new agreement with the IMF steered the Balaguer administration away from the reflationary policies it had pursued from 1986 onwards and towards further cuts in public spending. This could only result in continued conflict with state-sector workers.

Beyond the Lighthouse

The year 1992 marks a watershed for the Dominican Republic. Using the Columbus quincentennial as a pretext for a massive public relations campaign, the country is seeking to project an international image as a stable democracy with thriving new industries and investment potential.

1992 also sees the creation of the Single European Market, and the Domincian government is hoping that its membership of the Lomé Convention will allow it to diversify exports away from over-dependence on the US. Speaking in Santo Domingo in October 1991, the EEC representative predicted that the Dominican Republic could become a bridge for trade between Europe and the Americas, since it enjoys the preferential access accorded by both Lomé and the Caribbean Basin Initiative. As moves towards greater Caribbean integration and cooperation gradually materialise, the country has the opportunity to lessen its historic isolation from the non-Spanish speaking Caribbean. Yet, relations with Haiti remain a stumbling-block to its acceptance into the non-Spanish Caribbean community and full membership of CARICOM.

The year is likely to be a turning-point in another sense as the Balaguer era draws to a close. Already the struggle for succession is under way within the ruling party, while the PRD believes itself ready to return to power after years of marginalisation. The popular movement will play a central role in the process of post-Balaguer political change, even if the precise form it takes remains unpredictable. As long as the poor of the *barrios* and countryside remain excluded from the political system, the future will be one of continued conflict and economic decline. If, on the other hand, a more participatory political culture evolves, escaping from the traditions of *caudillos* and clientilism, a generation of grassroots activists and organisers can offer the impetus for real change.

Observers and participants alike are undecided as to how the popular movement can best influence the course of political change. Some argue that the movement should continue to act primarily as a pressure group on the government, pushing for specific reforms to the benefit of the poor. Others, however, envisage a more direct role for the popular movement, encompassing participation in some form of broad based government. Most are agreed that the movement's most significant contribution to Dominican politics lies in its sense of grassroots democracy, divorced from the cynicism of the conventional party system.

The Dominican Republic has little experience of democracy. The ephemeral Bosch presidency of 1963, marred by indecision and uncertainty, was the closest approximation to a democratic regime in the country's history. In the thirty years since the end of the Trujillo dictatorship, authoritarianism and corruption have dominated political life. But these conditions have not prevented the growth of popular organisations whose potential, if not actual achievements, is enormous. Ultimately, the future of Dominican democracy lies with the poor of the shantytowns and rural communities who make up these organisations. Only with their inclusion in the developing political process can the Dominican Republic hope to move forward from its seemingly endless crisis.

Bibliography

Americas Watch (1989), *Haitian Sugar Cane Cutters in the Dominican Republic*. New York, Americas Watch

Americas Watch (1991), *Half Measures: Reform, Forced Labor and the Dominican Sugar Industry*. New York, Americas Watch

Ian Bell (1981), *The Dominican Republic*. Boulder CO, Westview Press

Jan Knippers Black (1986), *The Dominican Republic: Politics and Development in an Unsovereign State*. Boston, Allen & Unwin

Juan Bosch (1966), *The Unfinished Experiment: Democracy in the Dominican Republic*. London, Pall Mall Press

Juan Bosch (1990), *El PLD*. Santo Domingo, Alfa & Omega

Pedro Catrain (1991), 'República Dominicana: un sistema político inmóvil?' *Nueva Sociedad*, Caracas, no 115

Catherine M. Conaghan and Rosario Espinal (1990), 'Unlikely Transitions to Uncertain Regimes? Democracy Without Compromise in the Dominican Republic and Ecuador'. *Journal of Latin American Studies*, Cambridge, vol 22, part 3

Consultoras Asociadas (1989), *Zonas francas y mano de obra femenina en el Caribe: el caso de la República Dominicana*. Santo Domingo

Robert Crassweller (1966), *Trujillo: The Life and Times of a Caribbean Dictator*. New York, Macmillan

CRESDIP (1991), *Ayiti-República Dominicana: au seuil des années 90*. Port-au-Prince, CRESDIP

John T. Cuddington and Carlos Asilis (1990), 'Fiscal Policy, the Current Account and the External Debt Problem in the Dominican Republic'. *Journal of Latin American Studies*, Cambridge, vol 20, part 2

Carmen Diana Deere *et al* (1990), *In the Shadows of the Sun: Caribbean Development Alternatives and US Policy*. Boulder CO, Westview Press

Thomas Fiehrer (1990), 'Political Violence in the Periphery: The Haitian Massacre of 1937.' *Race and Class*, London, vol 32, no 2

Eugenia Georges (1990), *The Making of a Transnational Community: Migration, Development and Cultural Change in the Dominican Republic*. New York, Columbia University Press

François Girault (1983), 'Elections et progrès vers la démocratie en République Dominicaine (1978-1986)'. *Problèmes d'Amérique Latine*, no 89

Piero Gleijeses (1978), *The Dominican Crisis: The 1965 Constitutionalist Revolt and American Intervention*. Baltimore, Johns Hopkins University Press

GRIPAC (1990), *Por un movimiento social y popular alternativo*. Santo Domingo, GRIPAC

Jonathan Hartlyn (1991), 'The Dominican Republic: The Legacy of Intermittent Engagement'. Abraham F. Lowenthal (ed), *Exporting Democracy: The United States and Latin America*. Baltimore, Johns Hopkins University Press

Edward S. Herman and Frank Brodhead (1984), *Demonstration Elections: US-staged elections in the Dominican Republic, Vietnam, and El Salvador*. Boston, South End Press

Vanna Ianni (1987), *El Territorio de las masas: espacios y movimientos sociales en República Dominicana, abril 1984-abril 1986*. Santo Domingo, Editora Universitaria

Vanna Ianni (1990), 'De la democracía dominicana'. *Ciencia y Sociedad*, Santo Domingo, vol 15, no 1

Michael J. Kryzanek and Howard J. Wiarda (1988), *The Politics of External Influence in the Dominican Republic*. New York, Praeger

Lawyers Committee for Human Rights (1991), *A Childhood Abducted: Children Cutting Sugar Cane in the Dominican Republic*. New York, Lawyers Committee for Human Rights

Maurice Lemoine (1985), *Bitter Sugar*. London, Zed Books

Pablo A. Mariñez (1984), *Resistencia campesina, imperialismo y reforma agraria en República Dominicana (1899-1978)*. Santo Domingo, CEPAE

Pablo A. Maríñez (1988), 'Las Fuerzas armadas en la República Dominicana: profesionalización y politización.' Augusto Varas (ed), *La Autonomía militar en América Latina*. Caracas, Nueva Sociedad

John Bartlow Martin (1966), *Overtaken by Events: The Dominican Crisis from the Fall of Trujillo to the Civil War*. New York, Doubleday

José Moreno (1970), *Barrios in Arms: Revolution in Santo Domingo*. Pittsburgh, University of Pittsburgh Press

José Moreno (1986), 'Economic Crisis in the Caribbean: From Traditional to Modern Dependency: the Case of the Dominican Republic'. *Contemporary Marxism*, San Francisco, no 14

Frank Moya Pons (1980), *Manual de historia dominicana*. Santiago, Universidad Católica Madre y Maestra

Manuel Núñez (1990), *El Ocaso de la nación dominicana*. Santo Domingo, Alfa & Omega

Magaly Pineda (1990), *'La Vida mía no es fácil': la otra cara de la Zona Franca*. Santo Domingo, CIPAF

Roger Plant (1987), *Sugar and Modern Slavery: A Tale of Two Countries*. London, Zed Books

G. Pope Atkins (1981), *Arms and Politics in the Dominican Republic*. Boulder CO, Westview Press

Esteban Rosario (1988), *Los Dueños de la República Dominicana*. Santo Domingo, Editora Búho

Christian Rudel (1989), *La République Dominicaine*. Paris, Karthala

Adriano Sánchez Roa (1989), *Campesinos, crisis agropecuaria e inflación*. Santo Domingo, IMOC

Adriano Sánchez Roa (1990), *Los Dueños del café: 30 años de economía cafetalera*. Santo Domingo, IMOC

J. David Stanfield (1989), 'Agrarian Reform in the Dominican Republic'. *Searching for Agrarian Reform in Latin America*. Boston MA, Unwin Hyman

Ramón Antonio Veras (1983), *Inmigración, Haitianos, esclavitud*. Santo Domingo, Editora Taller

Linda M. Whiteford (1991), 'Debt Crisis, Birth Crisis'. *Hemisphere*, Miami, vol 3, no 2

Howard J. Wiarda and Michael J. Kryzanek (1982), *The Dominican Republic: A Caribbean Crucible*. Boulder CO, Westview Press

Index

The Latin America Bureau is a small, independent, non-profit-making research organisation established in 1977. LAB is concerned with human rights and related social, political and economic issues in Central and South America and the Caribbean. We carry out research, publish books, and establish support links with Latin American and Caribbean groups. We also brief the media, run a small documentation centre and produce materials for teachers.

BOOKS FROM THE LATIN AMERICA BUREAU
Faces of Latin America
Duncan Green

From Argentina to Venezuela, **Faces of Latin America** looks at some of the key actors in the region's turbulent politics -the military, the guerrillas, indigenous peoples, the Church and the women's movement,

The book also celebrates the vibrant culture of Latin America's peoples while tracing the roots of the continent's most pressing issues — underdevelopment and poverty, the environmental crisis, and the fight for democracy.

'This is an indispensable introduction and source of reference — and a sound debunking of almost every previous misconception about the region.'
Amanda Hopkinson, *New Statesman and Society*

'Duncan Green has humanized our neighbours without sentimentalizing them. Clearly the work of an author who knows Latin America — and cares.'
Richard Fagen, Stanford University

1991 224 pages ISBN 0 906156 59 9 £10.00/US$18.00

Columbus: His Enterprise
Hans Koning

Examines the personality and motivation of a man who changed the course of history. Exploding the myth of the Great Navigator, the author reveals how Columbus accidentally found a continent and systematically pillaged its resources.

'...well argued, refreshing and worth stating' Hunter Davies, *Literary Review*

'Makes fascinating reading... should be compulsory.' Christopher Hill, *New York Review of Books*

1991(UK edition) 144 pages ISBN 0 906156 60 2 £5.75

US edition published by Monthly Review Press, New York

Grenada: Revolution in Reverse
James Ferguson

The US invasion of Grenada in October 1983 marked the final demise of four years of revolution, already derailed by internal strife. Heralded by the Reagan administration as a victory for freedom, it offered US technocrats the chance to turn the island into a model of free-market prosperity.

Revolution in Reverse reveals the extent of the failure of the US model — economic and political — in Grenada and the impact of that failure on the island's people.

'...offers a wealth of hard information and incisive observation.'
Rickey Singh, *Caribbean Contact*

'A must for anyone interested in, or living in, the Caribbean.'
Daily News, New York

1990 160 pages ISBN 0 906156 48 3 £5.75/US$9.50

Far From Paradise
An Introduction to Caribbean Development
James Ferguson

Traces Caribbean history from Columbus to the present day, looking at slavery, the colonial period, the struggle for independence and the rise of US regional influence. Questioning the official concept of development, it also examines the recent experiences of four Caribbean nations — Jamaica, Grenada, Trinidad & Tobago and Haiti.

'A fascinating introduction'
The Independent

'Essential reading for all who teach the history, politics and geography of [the Caribbean].'
Times Educational Supplement

1990 65 pages,large format ISBN 0 906156 54 8 £5.75/9.50

Prices are for paperback editions and include post and packing.

LAB books are available by post from Latin America Bureau, 1 Amwell Street, London EC1R 1UL. Cheques payable to LAB. Write for a free catalogue.

US$ orders for LAB books should be sent to Monthly Review Press 122 West 27th Street, New York NY10001. Cheques payable to Monthly Review Press.